ESSAYS ON JUNG AND THE STUDY OF RELIGION

Edited by

Luther H. Martin and James Goss

UNIVERSITY
PRESS OF
AMERICA

LANHAM • NEW YORK • LONDON

Copyright © 1985 by

University Press of America,® Inc.

4720 Boston Way
Lanham. MD 20706

3 Henrietta Street
London WC2E 8LU England

Library of Congress Cataloging in Publication Data
Main entry under title:

Essays on Jung and the study of religion.

    Selection of papers originally presented to a
"Consultation on Jungian psychology and the study of
religion" at the 1979-1981 Annual Meetings of the
American Academy of Religion.
    Includes bibliographies.
    1. Religion—Study and teaching—Congresses.
2. Psychology, Religious—Study and teaching—
Congresses. 3. Juing, C. G. (Carl Gustav), 1875-1961—
Influence—Congresses. 4. Jung, C. G. (Carl Gustav),
1875-1961—Contributions in the study and teaching of
religion—Congresses. 5. Jung, C. G. (Carl Gustav),
1875-1961—Contributions in religious psychology—
Congresses. I. Martin, Luther H., 1937-   . II. Goss,
James, 1939-   . III. American Academy of Religion.
Meeting.
BL41.E87   1985   200'.1'9   85-17865
ISBN 0-8191-4923-3 (alk. paper)
ISBN 0-8191-4924-1 (pbk. : alk. paper)

TABLE OF CONTENTS

iii

TABLE OF CONTENTS continued

EDITORS' PREFACE

> . . . religion is not only a sociological and
> historical phenomenon, but also something of
> considerable personal concern to a great number
> of individuals.
>
> --C. G. Jung (CW 11, 1)

The essays collected in this volume are selected
from papers originally presented to a "Consultation on
Jungian Psychology and the Study of Religion" at the
1979-1981 annual meetings of the American Academy of
Religion. We convened this consultation to initiate
dialogue between those scholars concerned with the
academic study of religion and those concerned with
this major psychological thinker who had concerned
himself so centrally with the question of religious
meaning.

The first group of papers in this volume present
four differing views on Jungian psychology and the
study of religion. Ann Ulanov, from the perspective
of a Jungian analyst, argues that Jung's psychological
hermeneutic can link the archetypal meaning of
religious expressions, which have their own history,
to the immediate psychological experiences both of the
scholar and of the student. Peter Homans, on the
other hand, locating Jung in his psychological and
cultural context, questions whether Jung's
epistemological shift from the social and traditional
to the inner and personal, in fact, offers a
non-reductive way to translate traditional Christian
images into a psychological terminology acceptable to
modern man, or whether it, rather, explains
traditional Christianity away.

William Paden and Luther Martin, like Homans, are
concerned to situate Jung's thought. Whereas Paden

locates Jung's central concern with religion in the history of ideas context of European phenomenology of religion and its concern for the integrity of religious data, Martin describes Jung's psychology out of a history of religions context as being fundamentally influenced by gnostic imagery and its concern for universal meanings.

The second group of papers collected represent the two areas of religious study which Ulanov suggested most benefit from a Jungian hermeneutic: the understanding of texts (Wayne Rollins, James Goss, Mokusen Miyuki) and the history of religions (Luther Martin).

Rollins surveys the place of scripture in the life and work of Jung and reminds the scholarly community that religious texts are not only a product of historical, social, theological, literary, and linguistic traditions, but also are a product of the images, visions, and truths of the soul. Similarly, Goss employs Jungian insight to complement a post-Bultmannian understanding of the eschatological significance of Jesus's proclamation of the Kingdom of God. Since both Jung and Bultmann agree that mythological language is in some sense language about the self, a Jungian perspective helps enrich, in Goss' view, the post-Bultmannian discussion because of Jung's primary concern to preserve the figurative or imagistic sense of religious language.

Miyuki's interpretation of the ancient Buddhist Legend of Ajatasatru illustrates the possibilities of a Jungian hermeneutic for interpreting non-Western texts, an area explored by Jung himself in his collaboration with Richard Wilhelm but largely neglected by contemporary scholarship. It also suggests implications of a Jungian perspective for the comparative study of religion.

Martin is concerned with the possibilities of a Jungian perspective primarily for the heuristic and pedagogical work of historians of religion. Employing the complex example of Hellenistic religions, he concludes that a Jungian perspective suggests insights into the collective or socio-historical dimension of mythological images and structures which are only hinted at by traditional scholarship.

We decided to focus the final meeting of the

consultation upon some implications of James Hillman's post-Jungian "archetypal psychology" for religion. The third group of contributions were selected from the presentations to this meeting.

James Hall offers a helpful discussion of the differences between Jung and Hillman, while rejecting most of Hillman's revisions of Jung. His primary objection is that Hillman's archetypal psychology stresses the phenomenology of the unconscious in Jung's writings at the expense of Jung's lifelong scientific and clinical concerns also for the importance of consciousness.

Thomas Moore, on the other hand, proposes an analysis of scholarship itself, based upon Hillman's amplification of the anima image. Recalling some of Ulanov's concerns, he feels that religious scholarship has become disconnected from the inner lives of people, whereas "anima scholarship" could restore this connection. Similarly, Walter and Mary Brenneman find Hillman's amplification of archeytpes the most helpful for their study of Irish-Celtic myth.

Finally, David Miller suggests a mediating position between Jung and Hillman situated in a poetic-theological perspective on "between-the-times."

We hope these essays will stimulate further discussion among those who have special interests in the psychology of Jung and its possibilities for the academic study of religion as well as among those with more general interests in the theoretical and methodological issues associated with the study of religion. We hope, too, that students approaching these issues for the first time might be directed towards the personal and intellectual possibilities offered both by Jung and by the study of religion, and to the broader historical and theoretical concerns to which these possibilities belong.

Two articles in the volume have had a previous publication history. Peter Homan's work appeared in a slightly different form in Jung in Context published by The University of Chicago Press, and used here by permission. The paper by James Goss was published in The Journal of the American Academy of Religion, XLIX, pp. 363-381.

The editors wish to express their gratitude to

Robert Lawson, Vice President for Research and Dean of the Graduate College of the University of Vermont, and to Jerome Richfield, Dean of the School of Humanities at California State University, Northridge for providing funds to help with the preparation of this book for publication. In addition, we wish to thank Rux Martin for her valuable editorial contributions, and Märta Lawson, typist.

SECTION I

PERSPECTIVES ON JUNGIAN PSYCHOLOGY

AND THE STUDY OF RELIGION

1

CHAPTER 1

IMAGE AND IMAGO:

JUNG AND THE STUDY OF RELIGION

Ann Belford Ulanov

Jung's investigation of the human psyche has had
an extraordinary and far-reaching impact on the
twentieth century. To assess the implications of his
work for the study of religion, we must begin where
Jung began and ended, with Jung the clinician engaged
in psychotherapy with specific persons.1 Clinical
work and clinical focus on the effects of specific
psychic images, manifested in the dreams, complexes,
symptoms and defenses of specific persons form the
basis of Jung's research and anchor his far-flung
speculations about human belief-systems and processes
of transformation.

A clear example of what I am talking about is
Jung's recovery to collective consciousness of
alchemy. Here, for him, was a serious endeavor,
occupying some of the best minds for over seventeen
centuries, but considered nonsense in our own century
and for several preceding it. He saw there in
abstruse chemical operations significant efforts at
the transformation of human being and of the world's
being. Jung was drawn to alchemy, not as an exotic
solipsistic fancy, but as a world of endless parallels
to the processes of human individuation. Another
example is to be found in Jung's investigations of
Christian dogma as it is reflected, for example, in
the mass, the doctrine of the trinity, the problem of
theodicy. Again, his understanding here springs
directly from his work with patients and with images
evinced in his own psychology. Scholars using Jung's

insights or methods must always remember the clinical basis of his work. Failure to do so is perilous for any attempt to make use of Jungian theory.

Image and Imago

As a clinician, Jung devised methods which deal with the psyche in its own modes of self-expression--through images. This approach strongly emphasizes the objective existence of the psyche as real, as there. The psyche addresses us. It has something to say and a language in which to say it. Jung conceptualized this experience of the psyche as living and autonomous--as other than consciousness though inclusive of it--in his term the objective psyche.2 What he means by that is a presence of unconscious mental processes intimately bound up with a life of the instincts antecedent to the growth of the conscious ego. This life of autonomous and spontaneous instinct is the primordial stuff out of which the human ego emerges. Jung saw the objective psyche as existing in all persons, regardless of cultural, historical, social, political, sexual, racial, or religious differences. If we really wish to hear what this level of human psychic process addresses to us, we must learn its language and accept it on its own terms. We must not approach it as simply a language to be translated into our own and understood as we understand our own.

A major difference between Freud's and Jung's approaches to the psyche focuses on just this point. Freud approaches the unconscious from the point of view of consciousness and translates its free-flowing primary-process thinking into the terms of secondary-process thinking characterized by logic, verbal concepts, laws of contradiction and so forth. Freud then gives us the helpful concepts of ego, id, and superego that exchange energy according to principles of reality and pleasure. Jung, in contrast, tries to deal directly with the language of the unconscious, and thus gives us such notions as the shadow, the anima, the persona.3 Such odd, sometimes even comic terms, account in part for the deep suspicion in which Jung is held by some sections of the psychoanalytic community. Remember, for example, radio's Lamont Cranston, whose melodramatic moments were always identified by the announcement, "The Shadow knows what evil lurks in the heart of men. . . ." It seems sometimes as if Jung has gone over

3

entirely to the other side, the unconscious one, at the expense of reason. These symbols seem to be used then only in a detached verbal way and appear to reasonably normal persons as so much jargon, relentlessly typing actual experiences according to some pre-fabricated and not quite rational scheme.4

Jung stands out from other theorists of the psyche by his central emphasis on images, for it is through images we hear what the objective psyche wants to say to us. The language of the psyche is archetypal images which express the felt meaning of the instincts.5 Through these images we wrestle with the problems that beset us and through them we glimpse the way to seek healing. Through these images we experience healing, discover sometimes blessed insights, see conflicts end, gather our energies into new forms which become available to us for living in the world around us in relation to people around us.

By image Jung means something specific, what might be called a fantasy-image, not a psychic reflection of an external object, but rather an image depending on unconscious fantasy-activity, the product of which appears in consciousness, and often with startling abruptness. The image arrives. We receive it into ego-awareness. It appears to us, it enters our consciousness. We do not produce it or conclude with it, though we must work very hard to lay the ground for its appearance. We cannot construct it or manufacture it, though we can participate in its becoming. At higher levels of development this participation is essential, even if never conclusive for our understanding.

Great psychological value clings to fantasy-images. They elicit emotional reactions from us. They engage us by enraging us, by disgusting us, moving us to tears, to awe, to reverance, to perplexity, but always with some degree of fascination.6 The image grips our attention, even invades us, as for example in obsessive fantasies. The image is complex, yet has a quality of wholeness about it and its own serious autonomous purpose. "The image," Jung says, "is a condensed expression of the psychic situation as a whole."7 Not only does it reflect the unconscious contents that are momentarily brought together ("constellated" in the Jungian vocabulary), but also the immediate conscious situation that has stimulated the unconscious in response to some contents and inhibited it in response to others. Any grasp of the meaning of the image, therefore, must include the relation of conscious and unconscious and not leave either of them out. An image, then, cannot just be taken at face value, but must be entered into, wrestled with, linked up with our conscious thoughts, feelings, and values.

A personal image expresses the contents of what Jung calls the personal unconscious and of the personally-conditioned conscious situation.8 The image often conveys private significance to its owner without expressing much meaning for anyone else. A primordial archetypal image will touch a shared level of human experience, common not only in the present but across history.9 It will give a personal tone to "certain ever-recurring psychic experiences;" it expresses a living process and "gives a co-ordinating and coherent meaning both to the sensuous and to the inner perceptions, which at first appear to be without either order or connection. . . ."10 The image thus liberates energy for conscious inspection, meditation, and eventual use. It also links energies to a definite meaning, one which serves to guide action along the path that corresponds to the meaning. It loosens dammed-up energies by transforming natural instincts into mental structures. This kind of image is vital and immediate. It can form the dynamic basis of an idea based upon it. In other words, focus on images not only does not exclude the development of ideas, it may hasten and deepen them.

Images that arrest our attention, intrude on our behavior, and shape society take on a role Jung calls that of the imago. The imago combines personal and archetypal images into one dynamic unity. An imago inhabits an interrealm between subject and object that expresses the subject's experience of the object.11 For example, a child's experience of a parent is constructed of many elements--perceptions of what is actually there in the parent, subjective reactions of the child to the parent, projections of the child of its own good and bad feelings onto the parent, and archetypal associations to its mother or father. The resulting imago inhabits the space between the actual outer other--the parent--and the inner experience of the subject. The imago is, then, a large gathering-place for the many aspects of the object, for the subject's response to the object, for conscious experience and the unconscious projection

5

onto the object, and for archetypal images evoked by the experience of the object. All of these combine to form the rudimentary layers of a symbolic image that represents the meeting and interpenetration of these multiple levels of reality. To recognize the imago-world means having the ability to develop an authentic symbolic life.

The inner and outer levels of our life are bridged by symbolic images that comprise a distinct realm of reality in themselves. They act as the intercessory agents for consciousness, representing the symbolic value to the subject of the interpenetration of spheres of reality. For example, to a child on one level his mother is altogether "his" in the sense of belonging to himself and being directly connected to a host of subjective reactions, needs, impulses, and feelings in the child's emotional and spiritual world. On another level, the mother is herself, moving in her own world objectively, a world which the child perceives as "other," as belonging to the mother alone. On still another level, she stands for the archetypal world of the mother, embodying in her concrete person some several aspects of that primordial brooding presence. The combined parts of these perceptions and images make up the child's mother-imago. An adult conscious of such a mother-imago still operating can discover through it aspects of self, of the woman who is his mother, and of the mother archetype per se. Consciousness of the imago leads to wider awareness of self, of actual other person, and of the dimension of otherness.12

We can transpose this concept into the world of religious studies, with some excellent results, I think, just as Jung found in his investigation of the God-image or God-imago. Here, too, the image of God we investigate in our own field of religious study, or in our own religious experience, is made up of several layers. On one level it points to all those impulses, needs, fears, longings for protection, and desires for unity that we connect and project to the God-image. Inevitably, at least in part, it must express the subjective contents that we project onto the image--what Freud called our wish-God.13 Freud stopped here in his analysis. But the God-image also includes all that other world belonging to God that breaks into our world as truly objective, as addressing us, blessing us, summoning us. Both these levels are contained in Scripture and the texts of

6

faith--theologies, histories of thought and histories of symbol and myth that exist objectively in documents and worshiping communities. This is a whole world of secondary-process thinking that Freud overlooked in his analysis of religion, making a straight and exclusive line as he did from the fantasy of the believer to belief, excluding texts, history, and a whole structure of documented experience.

We go to another level when we examine images of God from the point of view of the primordial, looking to see which archetypes they embody and inspecting all their many greatly contrasting aspects. Cassirer's reference to Usener's notion of "momentary gods" is useful here as a corroboration of method and concept.14

Focusing on images this way gives a clinician certain advantages which have exact counterparts in the study of religion. For example, I can review my patients' material with a view to the regnant images operative in each one's psychology. Jung's emphasis on images gives me as a clinician a distinct approach to diagnosis and prognosis, not necessarily an exclusive approach or one that competes with other systems, but certainly always a supplementing one of high value. The same is true for those who adopt this approach in the study of religions.

Any analytical system or theory ultimately must offer finely made metaphorical nets to throw over the living data. Whether we speak of the introjected objects of Guntrip and Klein, or the dynamic deployment of energy in the id, ego, and superego systems of Freud, or the bombardment of stimuli upon the narcissistic wound and border-line defense system of Kohut and Kernberg, we are talking in pictures, in images that shine through even the most complicated and abstruse theoretical formulations. The advantage of Jung's approach is to go directly to the images the psyche offers us about its own condition. Thus, for example, instead of diagnostic labels for a person I may be working with, such as border-line, depressive, schizoid, obsessive, etc., I may think of my patient as occupied with a cluster of recurring gun images--guns that do not work because the bullets are the wrong size, or the firing pin is missing, because the trigger is broken, or the marksman's aim is off. A person who feels himself to be split into a right half and a left half may be involved in this set of images, one whose right half is collapsing while his left half is reduced to chaos and is drenched in pain. Images of right and left, which often superimpose themselves on other metaphors, come to be ways of describing perception, or fear, or suffering from different ends of the psychic spectrum.

Images may come in our dreams and remain with us. Recurrent motifs may last sometimes for decades: there we are once again for the hundredth time in that old childhood room; there we are once again being pursued by a mysterious stranger; there we are looking anxiously for a bathroom and when we find one and the toilets do not work, or are occupied, or are overflowing. Or, let us take a dream in the life of a patient. The dreamer is invited to a momentous viewing where he watches a cliff face being blown up, only to reveal an inner city that had been constructed over a long time and can only now be shown. A wondrous sight, but with a flaw, an upsetting, disturbing flaw. Though the dreamer is protected from the blast, some of the workers are not, and there lies before him now the badly mangled and bleeding body of a woman. The dream poses a crucial pair of problems--how to uncover the city without hurting any part of the psyche and how to protect the woman.

Approaching psychic material in this way, through central images of this kind, gives advantage to both analyst and patient. Judgement is softened. For no matter how skillfully used, other schemes almost always employ developmental theory which inevitably brings judgement with it--that one is only at a beginning level of development and not yet making much progress to maturer levels. One is seen and sees oneself only in terms of those stages. The temptation to moralize about where one should be by this time is almost irresistable. In addition, one can feel labeled by a concept--narcissistic, border-line, obsessive-compulsive. The immediate I, alive and here in particular, feels fitted to an abstract, generalized and pathological category. The image, on the other hand, does not judge me, but rather engages me. It is personal, particular; it comes out of me. The problem, to recall one dream metaphor, is how to get the gun working, if I like guns, or how to throw it away, if I do not like them.

Focusing on images changes the way we construct the prognosis of a case as well. Prognosis will

8

include relating to these images in a direct, immediate way. It is not just knowing about a condition and explaining it conceptually, nor, as Rank criticized Freud and Jung for doing, simply re-educating the patient in our own world-view. We must deal with the facts that have been dealt to us; we must accept and face the concrete images that inhabit us.

These images have their own character and unfold accordingly. Different from conscious rules that measure all data by fixed formulations, the psychic image has no such rules. Its world is not to be seen as arbitrary or chaotic, however. It possesses its own structure and to that we must pay close attention. Jung uses directed rather than free association for dream images, asking for example what in particular made your unconscious fetch this image of tiger into your fantasy, as opposed to a lion, or an elephant. Or, to take a patient's dream, why is a pale, wan, and wormy-looking female figure disgusting to you? Why this disgust and not one of many other kinds of response? Or, to go on to another dreamer, what is it specifically about a particular room that makes you keep dreaming of it, as opposed to all sorts of other rooms?

The image has its own structure and integrity. It may even be a false image or an evil one, such as the psalmist speaks of, but contained there, in its own vocabulary, is a specific kind of falsity to which we are subject; there is the specific kind of evil which is ours, which we do. For example, a man dreamt he was in a barn, in a boxstall. Small fuzzy little animals were sleeping around him, harmless, engagingly furry. "For some reason I take a stone and squash the animals. Why did I do it?" The dream calls his attention to gratuitous aggression in him and makes it possible to deal with it. Or, in another case, an image may correct a questionable sense of self: "I dreamt I was the pope but my crown kept slipping." Is the dreamer suffering from inferiority or superiority? Images of our false selves, our counterfeit selves, are part of our reality as are images that are false in the sense of not being quite exact because they do not include everything needed to see ourselves. They offer clues, hints, a fullness of detail, but no rational discourse about ourselves.

The image is inclusive, in its own way, of

9

conscious and unconscious purposes and values, of individual and social realities. Occasionally we experience one of those remarkable dreams where we see directly how an inner lack in ourselves gets translated into social attitudes. We see how in failing to live all of ourselves we over-emphasize another part of ourselves and how we enact that imbalance by exclusive emphasis on one part of social reality with an accompanying prejudice against other parts. In the rebellions of the 1960's a young man dreamt he and others were planning to bomb a college building when some "tight establishment types" came up for a tour of the building. The dreamer showed them around, waiting only until they left so he could set off the bomb. But before leaving, the establishmentarian pointed out to the dreamer where there were some old bombs under the building's floor boards, bombs left over from the war, and ready to go off and kill him. The dreamer consciously opposed people he labeled "establishmentarian." But his dream showed him he must listen to that part; it could save his life. Another dreamer, a man who emphasized the powers of reason to excess, in his dreams constantly encountered a small retarded boy holding out his arms to him. The image was pointing out to him that his over-emphasis on reason might be linked to fear of some part of himself that he experienced as retarded and uncomfortably dependent.

Somewhat differently, the collective social-political situation may evoke in us parts of our being that cannot otherwise come to life. The psyche for Jung, we must remember, is objective, and lives outside ourselves as well as within us. Depending on our temperament, we may be brought home to ourselves by the words of another person, or an image dominant in our culture, by group or family example, or through a political movement that causes to come into our awareness new elements of being that we would not have arrived at alone. In the world of religious studies the parallel sources of influence would be the power of the text, or the historical moment, or the confluence of social, economic, and political realities with an inner vision, as in the cases of Luther or Gandhi. New religious insights may make us see the birth of new symbols in our world. But always it is our conscious relation to the concrete, particular and lively psychic image that will bring new social forms alive to us and help retire restrictive old stereotypes or abstract formulas which deaden our sense of the concrete person. Take the present-day emphasis on feminist studies, for example. The issue here is inquiry into the concrete works and lives of women, and, at its best, concrete efforts to discover what images of female and feminine inhabit us, whether we are male or female. It is not, we hope, simply to replace old stereotypes about women with new ones.15 The new ones may reverse the old ones, but they may also act in equally confining and sadistic ways. We must ask ourselves in this context, what are the images that inhabit us, and which ones underlie what we read about the female or the male? If we can no longer so easily project the imagos onto the opposite sex, can we see these imagos and what they disclose as parts of ourselves? Will they lead us really to see more of the other, really to see the other, female or male?

On the more subjective side, the world of images and imagos offers individuals a space in which to meditate upon their experience of otherness--of self, of persons, of reality. In looking at the images which live within us, whether negative or positive, we open up to a space where we can take apart and recombine different aspects of our psyches--of a drive, of a desire, of a fear. By joining these semi-conscious levels with the exposed parts of reality, we help civilize our unconscious primitive material, taming its energies into liveable forms. In this sense such symbolic images act to transfer energies from crude to more refined forms. We develop the capacity to substitute a number of different kinds of objects for an original crude impulse, bringing the energy into play in a richly amplified form. What we are doing, which religious study must take very seriously into account, is constructing a relationship to the otherness of the symbol in concrete personal terms. These terms always include our actual ego identity, what might be called our worldly presence. We select different parts out of which we build the unities, those clusters of experience and understanding that give us a sense of life's meaning and reconcile us to its hardships and tragedies. Thus working with images constructs a spiritual relation to otherness, to self, to God.

It is precisely this concrete and lively relation to images that brings a person healing insights. It may be useful to know I have a conflict between a tyrannizing superego and a demanding id-life, but that

11

knowledge does not show me how to come to live with the conflict. A dramatic dream-image of a son, believing he must cut off his father's leg in order to save his sister's life, only to discover after performing the bloody amputation that it was not necessary and that now he must carry his father on his back, shows all the sides of the anger and anguish involved in the struggle. The concrete images can lead the dreamer to examine and relate to the underlying issues of the dream and to find another less perilous route to deal with them.

We find help in analytic notions of "narcissistic syndrome," "anxiety neurosis," help in tracing present illness to past failures in Winnicott's idea of the "facilitating environment." But we do not always find relief. The image makes the concept come alive, whether we are looking at it for psychoanalytical or religious purposes. The image gives expression to nondiscursive elements of suffering, gives visibility to hate we cannot bring ourselves to express, gives an outlet to the tension that seeks to be lived, and above all offers a way to live in the present, a relationship that will fill up the emptiness of a past relationship that has gone wrong or been left unlived.

Doing this sort of reconnecting has social, intellectual, and religious implications, for denial of the archetypal world may effect a denial of humanity. We become contaminated when there is unlived life in us, victims of an ego too frail to house and humanize the energy that flows through us. We then become a contaminant to others—stifling their feelings, cutting off their connections, discouraging their perceptions.

Implications for Religious Studies

Many precise parallels suggest themselves between Jung's clinical approach to the psyche and the task of the religious scholar. Studying the texts of religious faith is a special enterprise in the intellectual and the academic world. It is so as well—or at least should be—for the depth psychologist. We know these texts of faith were alive to people in the past. We do not always see how much they can mean to us in the present time. They speak of configurations of being and the human apprehension of them. They solicit participation of the reader and hearer of their words. The scholar, to be a scholar, must somehow enter into the meaning of these words and sense that lively faith at least imaginatively, if not with reverence, in order to understand his or her subject-matter at all. This aspect of the nature of religious studies poses special problems for the fate of the discipline. For if the scholar is too much detached from this immediate addressing of his or her own person by the text of faith then what is there will not be grasped at all. And yet if the scholar simply reads into the text his or her own journey of faith, or a parallel despair of ever finding faith, then what the text really does express will also be lost, but from the opposite side.

Like Jung's notion of the psyche as objective, as absolutely there, autonomous and quite other than consciousness, religious texts also speak from another point of departure. They purport to give voice to the word of God, or of being, speaking to us. We may hear in them a voice from another world beyond the grave, or from the non-ego reality that goes beyond our ego-world of self and society. Religious texts are texts of multiple mysteries. They present what is a radical otherness to our own familiar human world. Like Jung's objective psyche, possessing its own language of images with which to communicate to consciousness, the many different kinds of texts of faith speak in their own particular and even peculiar language. All of them draw heavily on image and symbol. Here Jung's work can greatly help scholars of religious texts, with his research into the history of symbols and with the enormous amount of sheer information he collected about the psychic meaning of specific images and symbols.16

Jung's hermeneutic is principally a psychological one: he links symbols to the living process of the psyche, emphasizing as no one else did the peculiar psychic meaning of symbols. He saw that they express the conscious and unconscious situation at any given moment, past or present, and convey to consciousness an energy that is otherwise inaccessible. Thus Jung opens to scholars the life-current of religious images by focusing on the psychic experience of doctrines, of faith-images, or god-images. These images express the living apprehension of the mystery of being in relation to the mystery of selves-in-development. Jung helps link up the timeless archetypal meaning of religious symbols to the immediate psychological experience of the scholar and the student.

A great problem in teaching, as we all know, is the deadness that so often threatens it. And so we remember with particular joy those times in our own learning when a subject came alive to us, bringing us a whole world of interconnected meanings. By reaching out to its life, we discovered something had quickened in ourselves. But we also must know after we taught a particular bit of material that glassy stare in students' eyes that communicates to us an unpleasant unuttered question: "So what?" We can see clearly that the knowledge has not penetrated or come alive for the students. As teachers of religion, it is this we shall have to answer for on Judgement Day—How could we take something so vitally alive as religion and make it so deadly dull in the teaching of it?

We may make our point understandable to our students but fail to connect it to anything alive in them. To bring it alive, we must touch the psyche—our own and our students'—by making a bridge between the image in the text and the images in the interpreter, in us. At the very least, then, students must come to see that faith is a life as well as a text. Though they need not believe in order to understand a text academically, their grasp of the text does depend on discovering how and what the writers and hearers of the text did believe. In the intellectual study of religious texts we do not seek to convert our students, but we must make clear to them that belief in something is possible and, further, that experiencing that possibility is intrinsic to grasping in any depth the meaning of a text of faith. Just as psychoanalytic theory cannot be understood without reference to the patients in relation to whom the theory is fashioned, we cannot understand religious texts without reference to the believers for whom these images conveyed the heart of being in its crucial otherness. The greater the perception of that fact, the more exciting the study of religion. The dimmer the perception, the larger the pitfalls of pedantry loom.

To know that as a scholar we must deal with the psychic meanings that stand behind what we study and teach is to close the escape hatch of schizoid splitting so typical of academics where heart and soul are left out of professional work. Such omissions contribute to the demise of religious studies and to their politicization as a desperate effort to revive

14

them.

To approach a text of faith as issuing from an
otherness and as bespeaking the Divine is often
rejected by teacher and student alike as too
threatening.17   One fears that the study of religion
will   degenerate   into   formless,   subjective
emotionalism--not, for example, what Augustine said
but how I feel about what Augustine said. This need
not be the case. Indeed the fear that it will be so
is like the patient's fear that recognition of the
objectivity of the unconscious as other than
consciousness will deliver an already fragile ego into
chaos.   Behind this fear lies the assumption that
conscious ordering is the only ordering that exists,
just as behind the scholar's fear lies the assumption
that a rational and logical ordering of study is the
only kind of possible ordering.

Jung's investigations of imagery offer reassuring
evidence that images, and hence the unconscious from
which they arise, offer their own kind of ordering, no
less structured or significant than rationality, just
constructed along different lines. An image rising
from the unconscious unfolds and includes things not
seen before. It proceeds to new insights. The task
is to connect its unconscious way with our conscious
way so as to have at our disposal both ways of
ordering.   For example, in a seminary course of
study--it could be in homiletics or philosophy of
religion or biblical studies--a student may discover
that his way toward grasping the image of the
Johannine God of love is blocked because he is
bypassing some spontaneous personal image of God that
resides in him.   One of my students dreamt he was
worshipping a pig; and really worshipping it, with
awe, fear and trembling. By acknowledging that image,
receiving it into his conscious awareness, not
identifying with it, but feeling its liveliness, its
otherness, and making a space for it, he found more
room in himself to apprehend the vitality and inner
dynamism of that image of God as love. The pig does
not replace it, nor does a chaos threaten. Instead, a
very distinct image appears, a pig that needs
investigation, meditation, and response.

In the study of religious texts, most of which
are image-laden, images will be touched off in
ourselves and our students. We need to make room for
them in order to get on with our work. To ignore them

15

is to deny our study a vital energy.

Similar to Jung's focus on images as providing a valuable diagnostic and prognostic tool, focus on the regnant images in a text of faith gives us a way to order our study of the history of a religion. Images unfold and lead to other images that, in conjunction with a literary, social and contextual situation, build up a history. For example, in studying the Old Testament, certain recurrent clusters of imagery turn up, as is also true in the New Testament. An interesting question to ask is what made some of the New Testament authors take up some dominant Old Testament images and christianize them, while omitting others. What was it about the images that determined their selection? This question does not exclude the valuable research into the literary and the contextual socio-political-economic situation that also contributed to the selection of certain images. But it adds to that research an inquiry into the images themselves--their archetypal bases and autonomous propensity to undergo transformation to new levels of differentiation in the human psyche under the influence of Christianity. A still more psychological way to ask the same question is, Were those images taken into Christianity images of the "true self," in Winnicott's language, and were those discarded seen as images of a "false self"?18

Jung's approach helps in both the subjective and objective tasks of the scholar of religion. On the objective side, new ways open to study texts' images of faith and the ways in which we hear God speak to us there and elsewhere. This emphasis recognizes the autonomy of the psychic image, its inherent vitality, and its power to shape the very structures of society that have apparently shaped it. This perspective supplements our conceptual work in clarifying the social contexts in which religious texts are written, in articulating systematically the truths of theology, philosophy, literature, and so forth. It does not replace those truths; it brings them alive. To find in Tillich's theology, for example, the dominant image of the boundary line, gives insight into his whole system and its method of correlation that seeks to bridge the boundaries of pairs of different realities--philosophy and theology, culture and faith, eternal symbols and existential situations. To find in Barth the sovereign image of Christ as mirror which reflects back to us our true image, makes immediate

sense of the subtleties of his theological method of
__analogia fides__.

This emphasis on images in the languages of faith
also reminds us that ours is a privileged study, that
in the larger world of scholarship we occupy a
particular place that others may dismiss as
woolly-headed, a bit mad, even deluded. But we know
it is a privileged study. We read the human records
of persons' experiences of truth, of reality, of that
which centers everything else, of that which __is__.
Focusing on the images in our texts not only gives us
an additional way to order those texts, but, parallel
to the healing effect of psychological insight, such a
focus opens us to the illuminating qualities of truth.
In this image or that, we find at least a bit of
central truth disclosed, offered, and addressing us
directly.

Awareness of such a fact imbues the scholar's
day-in, day-out work with unceasing vitality for
decades, perhaps for a lifetime. It sustains
scholarly work by assuring it of connection to
enduring truth. It protects us from becoming
burnt-out cases, dried-up relics. Here is the fire,
the water, the needed light, the deep darkness. We
need such a source to survive the rigors of academic
life, in order to do our teaching well in classrooms,
and to write with substance. For we perform two
functions: we convey information, and we act as a
bridge to the inner reality of faith in the texts we
study. Jung helps us in both tasks, enlarging our
information about images and quickening our ability to
convey their psychological meaning for our readers and
hearers. We thus reach, in Jung's language, both the
ego world of context and society, linguistic form and
political situation in which a religious text is
written or an image of God is upheld, and the
archetypal world of timeless images conveying
permanent truths. To avoid these images is to be
detoured into dry abstractions, killing the life, or
making the student hunt too hard to find it. We
commit our worst sins as teachers in this
respect—squashing in our students their love for
truth and their hunger to know that a lively durable
belief is possible. We bore them to death. As an act
of hostility that is bad enough, but in religious
studies it is even worse because we take the central
truths of God and cover them over, make them opaque
and dull. We set up impossible obstructions.

On the subjective side, Jung helps the scholar of religion by reminding us of the necessity to make more space in our own awareness for the images that inhabit us. Jung's emphasis on the psychic meaning of religious images addresses us as the persons we are—or fear to be—with the meanings we live by or have lost or still seek. This leads us to be aware of our students as persons. Whatever images inhabit us, they must affect our work and what work we are able to make commendable to others. So we need to pay attention to what sorts of images live in us, which ones thwart us, which ones are dead, which alive. Such awareness will increase our understanding of why we cannot finish a thesis or a manuscript. We may be forcing images and hence a specific channel for energy upon ourselves when in fact our energy is already alive and flowing in another river-bed. Knowing what images inform our own lives puts us in conscious touch with them, thus opening ways for them to live in the world. And so zest is added to our teaching, fostering the igniting of imagination in us and all around us.

Coming into awareness of these images within us means just that—awareness, not identification. My student should not say, "Ah ha!" as at last he comes to know he really is a pig-worshipper at heart, throwing over as sham all his old faith in the Christian God of love. That would be identification—now with something from the unconscious side as before he was too much identified with his conscious image of God. He needs both. We need both. Otherwise we fall into that particularly bad practice among religious scholars that gives psychology and Jung a bad name—projection.

We project our personal images onto the texts of faith and reduce its otherness down to our own personal experiences of the otherness of the unconscious. Two crunchy movements then develop—psychological personalism and psychological abstractionism. We put into the text our particular imagos and substitute them for the larger, more encompassing images of faith. My faith becomes all faith. We abstract from the particularity of a text by translating it into the terms of psychological jargon. A parable, for example, becomes nothing more than a joust between ego and shadow. We cease to make a bridge to the psychic meaning of the texts. Instead we replace it with a psychological formula which is too abstract to reach many people where they live. Or we replace the narrative of God's story with our own personal journey, not guessing at the mountainous inflation that act conveys.

At the opposite end of such dangers, we lose the personal dimension altogether. We disappear into the archetypal world, departing from the ego world of the flesh that God entered--the flesh of our bodies, of our time in history, our society and politics and economics and personal relationships. This is comparable to discussing the patient's imagery to the exclusion of the patient's real situation. We take up the images of faith but never find them incarnate in action, attitude, or devotion. We involve ourselves with images without reference to our relation to them, so that we now have many gods, as many as there are separate images. We resist the human task of uniting them. Instead we take our fragmented state, that was once such a problem, as the present solution. But this is identification psychologically and idolatry theologically. We identify with the psyche's capacity to produce images and make a god out of that.

No, we must have both worlds--the ego world and the archetypal. Only with both are we up to the strains of relating to the otherness that the texts of faith communicate and that our own images and imagos convey to awareness. We need a foot on both sides--an ego firmly enough rooted in its own reality to withstand opening and receiving the beyond-ego world without being swept away, an ego spacious enough to entertain these lively, even threatening images offered in the texts of faith which become tests of faith and demonstrations of faith as they call up images from within our own unconscious.

The scholarship and teaching of religion are not the same as analysis but then analysis is not the only way to enlarge consciousness and to feed the soul.

NOTES

1. Jung formulated his concepts on the basis of his work with patients, who can be roughly divided into two groups: those suffering from neurosis and those suffering from psychosis and confined to a psychiatric hospital. The majority of the latter group came from the lower strata of society, the former from the middle and upper strata.

2. For a summary of the meanings of this term, see C. G. Jung, _Two Essays in Analytical Psychology_, trans. R. F. C. Hull, _Collected Works_, Vol. 7 (New York: Pantheon, 1966), pp. 145ff; see also Ann Belford Ulanov, _The Feminine in Jungian Psychology and in Christian Theology_ (Evanston: Northwestern University Press, 1971), pp. 18-19.

3. For a longer discussion of these differences, see Ann and Barry Ulanov, _Religion and the Unconscious_ (Philadelphia: Westminster, 1975), pp. 65-68; see also pp. 26-32.

4. Particularly vulnerable to this criticism is Jung's notion of a man's anima or a woman's animus. People seem to find it harder to accept that we have a personification of the opposite sex living in us than they do an evil part, symbolized in Jung by the shadow. This may be due to the fear of sexual discrimination--that man and woman will be fixed in stereotypes--or it may result from sexual discrimination, e.g., the attitude that "No other sex part exists in me!" Generally we seem more comfortable with a shadowed part of ourselves that sabotages our actions with motives opposite to our conscious intentions than the more cross-grained textures of contrasexuality. To dream of a dark figure chasing us is not uncommon; hence it is not difficult to take that pursuit seriously as depicting an actual inner conflict. For a woman to dream of a negative animus figure--a

20

contemptuous judging man who berates her--and to accept that that attitude is actually her own, is less acceptable, more easily projected onto actual men in the world around her. For discussion of the anima and animus, see C. G. Jung, _Aion_, trans. R. F. C. Hull, Collected Works, Vol. 9,ii (New York: Pantheon, 1959), pp. 11-23, and Ann Belford Ulanov, Receiving Woman: Studies in the Psychology and Theology of the Feminine (Philadelphia: Westminster, 1981), Chapter 6 on "The Authority of Women."

5. An example of the way such an image expresses meaning is the following. A woman brought to her analytic session a dream about a big spider--the size of a dog--who appeared at her kitchen door. We worked on her associations to this spider image, which were mainly negative and emotional--fear, revulsion, panic at getting caught in the spider-web.

She associated to these feelings experiences with her own mother, feeling tangled in a web of her mother's manipulations that were delicate and hard to see but that nonetheless held her fast. She also felt imprisoned in her own negative reactions to her mother, unable to win through to the love that she felt for her mother as well. After talking in some detail about these feelings, I added that the spider was a symbol associated with the negative mother figure in its ensnaring activity and aggressiveness toward the helpless daughter. (The spider can symbolize the deathly womb of the Terrible Mother. See Erich Neumann, The Great Mother, trans. Ralph Manheim [Princeton: Princeton University Press, 1970], pp. 177, 184-185; C. G. Jung, Psychology and Alchemy, trans. R. F. C. Hull, Collected Works, Vol. 12 [New York: Pantheon, 1953], pp. 207f., figure 108 cited by Neumann, p. 177). The spider figure is associated with what the Indians call Maya, sitting in the center of her domain, eternally spinning her web of illusion. Yet the spider also symbolizes in a positive way the meeting of death and life, in their ceaseless alternation fundamental to the transformation of life, a sacrifice of the old for the building of the new. The spider who spins its web from out of its own body also symbolizes creative power.

Together, the dreamer and I hazarded an interpretation which ran along the lines of her finding herself in the dream, presented with, if not sought out by, an image that referred to her own negative experience of her mother. The interweaving of negative and positive forces in life, though terrifying, was also fundamental to her own transformation.

Fine. Or so we thought. But she came to the next session with the same dream image, now dreamt for a second time, except that in this dream she took the spider from her door, down the kitchen steps, across her backyard into a neighboring field and deposited it at some distance from her house. By the time she got home, barely inside the kitchen again, the spider appeared at the door, in effect knocking to be admitted.

This second dream told both the dreamer and me that the spider image in its personal and archetypal dimensions could not be so easily dealt with by interpretation, even a correct one. The unconscious repeated itself, as if to say, Clearly you did not get the point; so I'll say it again: this spider image wants to come into the kitchen! "Coming in" means more than understanding, however emotionally informed that understanding may be. In this case it means entering into the kitchen space of the woman's psyche and interacting with her there. The kitchen space touched on her own maternal experience as nurturing and feeding her five children, as well as on her ability to transform raw substances into edible and life-building forms. The spider image expresses a meaning yet to be discovered about her maternal instinct, a meaning that would particularly emerge out of admitting negative feelings and recognizing the inevitable mixture of the negative and the positive in life.

In retrospect, I see now an added line of interpretation I missed seeing then: the kitchen, in addition to referring to her actual room, could also symbolize the analysis where the work of transformation occurred, where she and I were being "cooked," so to speak. The reality of the multiple meanings of the spider needs to be admitted into the analytical relationship too.

All examples of psychological material, unless otherwise noted, are taken from my practice as a Jungian analyst, with thanks to those persons who allowed me to cite their experiences.

6. Images constantly turn up in people's dreams and fantasies as we all know but do not always admit. They include persons of all types, from the ordinary to the extraordinary. People known to the dreamer may appear--neighbors, colleagues at work, relatives, etc. People unknown and startling to the dreamer may also appear, a celebrity, a murderer bent on attacking the dreamer with a knife, a child whose helplessness and open love moves the dreamer to tears, a tramp who climbs into the back seat of the dreamer's taxi to grab a ride, a person of another culture, such as a Chinese woman or African warrior or Indian guru. In addition, part-images, human and inhuman, may take over fantasy and dream--such as an ugly wound whose jagged edges will not heal, or a blob of slime on the floor next to one's bed, or an abstract figure of lines and angles, or a vision of intense redness, or a bright yellow sun and deep blue sea. Animals, monsters, scenes of nature, even letters and numbers may come to us in images.

Images also occur spontaneously to people in activities other than dreaming, in praying, for example. For a discussion of this, see Ann and Barry Ulanov, _Primary Speech_: _A Psychology of Prayer_ (Atlanta: John Knox Press, 1982, Chapters 4 and 5). Images arise in teachers in the midst of presenting material to a class of students, in scientists struggling toward formulation of their findings. Images arrive when persons make love. Images can inhabit our pleasures and suffering. The images that confront us are as numerous and varied as we are ourselves.

7. C. G. Jung, _Psychological Types_, revised trans. R. F. C. Hull, _Collected Works_, Vol. 6 (Princeton: Princeton University Press, 1971), p. 442.

8. An unusual example of such a personal image is one presented to a young scientist in a dream the night before she saw her analyst for the first time. After a series of events involving the dreamer and the analyst, the dream concluded with the dreamer beholding with awe a revolving, luminous white, many-celled structure. This compelling figure reminded the dreamer of the design of cells she was examining in her research and the awe she felt in uncovering nature's secrets, discovering "how things work." Obviously, this image carries a specific personal meaning for the dreamer that derives from her vocation in the natural sciences.

9. An example of an archetypal image can be found in the scientist's dream of the previous footnote. Even though the image of the white, luminous structure in her dream recalled her own specific research, its composition of many cells connected to a center, its central importance to the whole dream, and its numinous effect upon the dreamer, both in the dream and on awakening, connect to the archetypal form of a mandala--that ancient Hindu design that combines the circle and the square achieving order within diversity, that Jung believed, from its repeated appearance in many patients' dreams, symbolized the center of the psyche.

10. C. G. Jung, _Psychological Types_, pp. 444-445.

11. Ann and Barry Ulanov, _Religion and the Unconscious_, pp. 224ff.

12. Jung gives an example of one of his own imagos in his description of his experience of his mother. For Jung, she possessed two personalities. Number one was the conventional, pastor's wife. Number two inhabited a pagan land, told strange tales, and uttered unconventional words. At the death of Jung's father she said to Jung, "He died in time for you." (C. G. Jung, _Memories, Dreams, Reflections_, ed. Aniela Jaffe, trans. Richard and Clara Winston. New York: Pantheon, 1963), pp. 48-49, 96. Jung's imago of his mother included, in addition to his personal experience of her, the archetypal theme of the dual mother, which he explored in detail in his _Symbols of Transformation_, trans. R. F. C. Hull (Princeton:

Princeton University Press, 1974), Vol. 5 of The Collected Works.

13. Images of God abound in people--ranging from negative ones of God as scolder, scorekeeper, punitive father, to positive ones of God as comforting mother, understanding friend, merciful Lord. Non-human images of God also turn up: God as cosmic blur, God as light, God as animal. For discussions of such images of God, see Anna Marie Rizzuto, The Birth of the Living God (Chicago: The University of Chicago Press, 1979), and Ann Belford Ulanov, "What Do We Think People Are Doing When They Pray?", Anglican Theological Review, Vol. LX, No. 4, October, 1978.

14. See Ernst Cassirer, Language and Myth, trans. Susanne K. Langer (New York: Dover, 1946), pp. 62ff.

15. For a discussion of the danger of old and new stereotypes, see Ann Belford Ulanov, Receiving Woman, Chapters 1 and 2.

16. See Ann Belford Ulanov, "Religion: Jung's View," International Encyclopedia of Psychiatry, Psychology, Psychoanalysis, and Neurology, ed. B. B. Wolman (New York: Human Sciences Press, 1977), Vol. IX, pp. 429-432.

17. See Ann Belford Ulanov, "The Christian Fear of the Psyche," Union Seminary Quarterly Review, Vol. XXX, Nos. 2-4, Winter-Summer, Summer, 1975.

18. See D. W. Winnicott, "Ego Distortion in Terms of True and False Self," in The Maturational Processes and the Facilitating Environment (New York: International Universities Press, 1965).

CHAPTER 2

C. G. JUNG: CHRISTIAN OR

POST-CHRISTIAN PSYCHOLOGIST?

Peter Homans

I. Introduction: Jung's (Two-Fold) Approach to Christianity

To the reader even moderately familiar with
Jung's writings, and for any reader guided by the
secondary literature on Jung, it is clear that
religion is a central theme in his mature work. In
his mature years Jung writes about religion again and
again, dealing with various aspects of it: primitive
religions and archaic man; Eastern religions; the
relation of psychotherapy to the work of the
clergyman; but above all about Christianity and
Christian dogma, in particular the dogma of the
existence or transcendence of God.

This feature of Jung's mature thought finds a
parallel in his personal life. The experience of
religion pervaded his turbulent childhood and early
adolescence.   During his psychoanalytic years
religious concerns colored his thinking about Freud's
work and the writing of Symbols of Transformation.
During the critical period described in his
autobiography as the time of "Confrontation with the
Unconscious" (1913-1918), he struggled with the
tension between traditional Christianity on the one
hand and modernity on the other hand. At the close of
this period (1918-1921) Jung wrote the first versions
of the Two Essays on Analytical Psychology,1 which
became a definitive statement of his major ideas, and

which outlined the structure of the individuation process. The individuation process became the center of Jung's mature thought. Later (from 1921 onward) he turned his mind back upon the phenomenon of religion, which had vexed him throughout so much of his early life, and interpreted it--or, rather, as I will explain shortly, re-interpreted it--according to his unique system of psychological ideas, all of which explicated the individuation process.

So, the question regarding Jung's relation to religion in the mature years is not whether it was a bona fide theme. Rather, the question is, given the fact that religion was a central theme, what was Jung's view of it? This question contains a central issue in understanding Jung's thought as a whole, one which has created many of the polarizations among critics of Jung, and can be explicated as follows. Did Jung, like Freud, develop a set of interpretive categories by means of which he could "see through" and thereby explain away traditional Christianity? Or, did he, in devising his system of unique ideas, conceive of a way to translate traditional Christianity into terminology acceptable to modern man, without appreciably altering the traditional doctrines? In other words, was Jung a Christian or a post-Christian psychologist?

The correct response to this question is that both aspects of it must be answered in the affirmative, but that neither one in itself comprises the whole of his approach. Jung did not opt for either of these alternatives in an exclusive manner. Rather, his thought on religion is a complex attempt to synthesize both. By applying the individuation process to traditional Christianity, Jung in effect created a double movement of reduction and retrieval of meaning. In one sense he was reductive: he interpreted the totality of Christian faith in the light of analytical psychology. This psychology became for him the key for "seeing through" the otherwise opaque character of the Christian faith. All the major tenets of Christianity were interpreted as instances of archetypes in the collective unconscious. The individuation process was the lens through which Jung viewed the Christian faith. It was a new set of categories, derived from his researches and his contact with Freud, completely foreign to the Christian tradition. Without this psychology that faith simply did not make any sense. Jung's interpretation of Christianity was in this sense very different from Christianity's own self-interpretation of itself. In this sense his psychology embodied what Paul Ricoeur has called a "hermeneutics of suspicion."[2]

But Jung's psychology contained a second movement, built upon the first, in which he attempted to retrieve religious meaning from the Christian tradition and incorporate it into his psychological theory of the person. Once the reductive movement had been made--once the psychological meaning of doctrine had been disclosed--then Jung proceeded to clothe these constructs with positive meaning and value, arguing that they were in fact essential if modern man, uprooted and dissociated from his traditional roots, was ever to re-relate himself to Christian tradition. Hence he claimed that the archetypes and the individuation process, while not part of the vocabulary of the traditional Christian, nevertheless captured the hidden essence of that tradition. Thus Jung's psychology contained within it, alongside its hermeneutics of suspicion, a "hermeneutics of affirmation." In order to emphasize the presence of a double movement in Jung's psychology, in which both rejection and affirmation were present, I call his approach a re-interpretation rather than simply one more interpretation. In all this Jung gave expression to an important facet of his personal identity--which existed alongside of that of originative psychologist and social critic--that of prophet or re-interpeter of traditional Christianity.

In proposing that a double movement was present in Jung's stance towards traditional Christianity, I am taking issue with existing discussions of Jung's view of religion. On the one hand there are the positively toned theological interpreters--such as Cox,[3] Schaer,[4] and V. White[5]--who have argued that his psychology is simply a re-statement in psychological terms of the principal tenets of the Christian faith. These writers have not given sufficient attention to the massive evidence which supports Jung's life-long struggle to repudiate Christianity--to free himself from its oppresive claims upon his life. Nor do they see the great extent to which Jung, in his mature writings, found traditional Christianity utterly incomprehensible. To say that a particular doctrine or tenet of faith is "really" an archetype of the collective unconscious is to assign to it a meaning quite different from that which the Christian tradition gives it.

On the other hand it is equally necessary--in order to achieve a correct and full sense of Jung's stance towards religion--to oppose the anti-Jungians such as Hostie,6 Philip,7 Rieff,8 and Johnson,9 who argue that Jung simply psychologized the Christian faith and in doing so completely secularized it. These critics have ignored the element of affirmation. They have not seen how classical Christian experience provided an absolutely essential matrix, or "field," or experiential context out of which the individuation process took its peculiar shape. Thus, for Jung, the traditional beliefs in God, Christ, the Trinity and the Church were all necessary background for the modern individual if he was to come to understand himself in a new way. Traditional Christianity was the indispensable context within which the individuation process could occur. Paradoxically, it was there in order to be put aside. In Jung's mind, analytical psychology evolved out of the Christian tradition, but the result was just as religious as was the context out of which it emerged.

It is helpful, in order to clarify this argument further, to point out that Jung's psychology was really comprised of three types of images of man. First, there was the good Christian, either Catholic or Protestant, who believed unquestioningly in the tenets of his faith and for this very reason was not needful of psychology. For such a person, traditional doctrine successfully organized unconscious processes and hence protected him from becoming neurotic. But Jung was primarily interested in a second type, the so-called modern man, who was fully self-conscious, rational and extraverted, who was oriented to science and the modern state, and who, because he was unconnected with the past, was vulnerable to the unconscious. And then there was the "Jungian man," who was modern in that he rejected the literalism and authoritarianism of traditional Christianity, but who also was in part traditional, in the sense that he was ready to reinterpret Christian symbols in the light of analytical psychology. Thus Jung's view of religion was complex: during his mature life he tried to weave his way through the tension between traditional religion and modernity and his psychology is an attempt--through its double movement of reduction and affirmation--to close the gap between what most people believe to be two unbridgeable orientations to the world.

This estimate of Jung's view of religion is clearly confirmed by the delineation of the individuation process found in the _Two Essays_. In that statement he defined the final stage of individuation as an encounter with a god-image which had a distinctly Christian cast to it. The consolidation of the archetype of the anima created a new sense of inflation, a merger with the deity which produced the feeling that "I and the Father are One."10 In order to come to terms with this merger, the patient could, Jung said, concretize or absolutize this image of God as "Father in Heaven."11 This would be the traditional Christian solution. But he cautioned against such a move, for to do so would only produce a new sense of moral inferiority and oppression—a fundamental prerequisite of traditional faith. In so saying Jung repudiated the Christianity of tradition and took the side of modern man, suspicious of all commitment to theological dogma. But he did not stop here. He went on to introduce the concept of the collective unconscious and the archetypes, in particular the archetype of the self, and to apply these interpretively to the theological situation. He spoke of the self not only as a mid-point between conscious and unconscious, but also as "the god within us."12 And he defined the emergence of the self as a natural and spontaneous process—which is to say it was not dependent on traditional theological dogma. Thus, by means of the categories of analytical psychology Jung was able first to repudiate traditional Christianity, and second to affirm the formation of the self as a genuine resultant of evolution out of the context of the initial theological situation.

Throughout his mature writings Jung never deviated from this approach to religion. True, he wrote a number of articles on Eastern religions, but his purpose in this was to emphasize what the West lacked. He did not share the interests of the historian of religion. Rather, he was predominantly concerned with the Christian faith. Through analytical psychology Jung reinterpreted traditional Christianity, first by repudiating its formulations, but then going on to show how the situation of classic faith provided the experiential matrix out of which the individuation process could evolve. Now, with this understanding of Jung's strategy firmly in hand, we briefly turn to his explicit writings on religion. While the basic strategy is present throughout all his many and varied analyses of religious questions, and provides the reader with a unified perspective upon their otherwise great diversity, it is particularly evident in his best-known work on the subject, Psychology and Religion.13 This text focusses Jung's central preoccupation: the psychological nature of the Christian doctrine of God.

II. The Themes of Suspicion and Affirmation in "Psychology and Religion"

At the very beginning of the book Jung set the stage for his basic strategy with regard to religion by distinguishing between religion on the one hand and dogmas or creeds on the other. He defined religion as "a careful consideration of certain dynamic factors that are conceived as powers: spirits, demons, Gods, laws, ideas, ideals. . . ."14 Religion, he wished to make clear, was an experience of a particular type--that is, it was immediate, subjective and therefore psychological. He equated it with what the Protestant theologian, Rudolph Otto, meant by "the numinous"--suggesting awe and reverence in relation to a supreme object. And later in the book he spoke of religious experience as "immediate experience"--by which he meant the experience of the irruption into an overly rational ego-consciousness of collective, archetypal material, an experience which in its own way inspires awe and dread or fear as well. In contrast to religious experience Jung juxtaposed dogmas and creeds. These were, he said, "codified and dogmatized forms of original religious experience."15 A dogma is formed when the immediate religious experience is congealed into a rigid and elaborate structure of ideas.

Thus, at the very outset of his book, Jung prepared the reader for his unique approach to religion. For dogma was the language of traditional Christianity, whereas religious experience was the target of analytical psychology. Jung's task was to unearth the structures and processes of religious experience, which dogma had obscured and repressed. By exposing the hidden roots of dogma, Jung would reductively interpret Christianity; but, by then demonstrating the underground source of dogma in universal religious experience, he would affirm and re-interpret traditional Christianity. The key to this double movement was the new system of ideas known as analytical psychology, and, in particular, the individuation process.

In order to carry his argument forward, Jung presented his readers with details of a practical case, several dreams of one of his patients in his psychotherapeutic practice. The life-situation of this dreamer was an important piece of Jung's argument. For he embodied Jung's concept of modern man: a scientifically-minded intellectual who, because of his commitment to modernity, could no longer believe in creeds and dogmas and who, furthermore, like most moderns, identified religion entirely with creeds and dogmatic tenets. Jung then analyzed these dreams and demonstrated that they contained images of the archetype of the quaternity, what he called a mandala. Such dreams reflected, he argued, the presence of immediate experience, of the numinous, and were religious in nature. they were, in fact, when properly interpreted, "symbols of God." Jung gave two further reasons for this conclusion. First, the comparative method had shown that ancient thinkers had associated quaternities with God. But Jung also suggested that mandalas were expressions of a religious attitude because the people who dream them link this symbol to the highest value in their personality. "Religion," he said, "is a relation to the highest and most powerful value . . . that psychological fact which wields the greatest power in your system functions as a god."16

Having established that dreams and vision of quaternities and mandalas were evidence of the presence of God in the experiential life of the subject, Jung was forced to reflect upon traditional formulations of the nature of the deity. He rightly turned to the doctrine of the Trinity as the privileged form in which the character of deity had been expressed in Christian faith. And he concluded that the Trinity, with its exclusive emphasis upon three rather than four elements in the divine life, was excessively rational and one sided. The doctrine of the Trinity had repressed the principle of evil and the principle of femininity from the nature of God, and hence also from the consciousness of man. The quaternity, on the other hand, made room for these elements and as such was a more complete and also fully natural symbol of the godhead. But Jung's major concern with the mandala was not simply with the Trinity per se--he discussed this at length in a separate essay on the subject--but also with what mandalas presaged for the fate of the image of God in the modern world.

In traditional Christianity the image of God existed external to the believer's psyche, and he submitted to and was reconciled with that imago. But in the mandala dreams of modern man, Jung said, "the place of the deity seems to be taken by the wholeness of man."17 Jung called this wholeness or totality of man the Self, the end result of the individuation process. The emergence on the modern scene of mandala dreams signified, it would seem, the disappearance of the traditional view of God and the appearance of the Self.

Once again Jung had brought into play what I have called the strategy of a double movement. By means of the categories of analytical psychology he was able to interpet psychologically the key Christian theological formulation of the nature of God. The image of God embodied in the Trinity was repressive, and it distorted psychological reality accordingly. Thus Jung reduced Christian theology to psychology in the spirit of a hermeneutics of suspicion. But then he went on to show how the reality of the deity, while no longer an object of traditional faith, continues to live in the form of a structure of the self, undergirding as it were "the wholeness of man." His point is reminiscent of his concept of the self as "the God within us" found in the Two Essays. By virtue of the interpretive power of analytical psychology, the self evolves out of the matrix of traditional faith. In such fashion did Jung attempt to retrieve meaning from the Christian tradition. Here is his hermeneutics of affirmation.

Toward the end of the book Jung introduced one of his most important concepts, "the withdrawal of projections," which illustrated with further clarity his strategy of a double attitude towards traditional Christianity.18 Primitive man lived in a state of almost total projection: he projected inner emotions onto external objects and persons and consequently lived in a condition of relatively minimal self-consciousness and self-knowledge. But as Western history progressed, it produced circumstances which brought the gradual withdrawal of projections and a

33

consequent increase in consciousness and knowledge of both self and world. Physical science caused the withdrawal of "the most distant projections." Echoing Max Weber's concept of disenchantment, Jung referred to this as the first stage in the despiritualization of the world. The early discoveries of modern science became the foundations of the modern outlook, shaping as they did an entire view of the world. According to Jung, it was the essence of modern man to examine all his projections. Modern man "cannot project the divine image any longer"[19]--that is, he is no longer able to believe in the existence of God, as described by the traditional dogmas of the church. While Jung did not mention Freud in this context, it is clear that the latter's psychology of religion epitomized this stance of modern man. Hence the impasse of modernity: modern man can no longer believe--he has withdrawn his projections--but when he does so, he becomes an isolated ego-consciousness. Jung resolved this conflict by adducing analytical psychology: "if we want to know what happens when the idea of God is no longer projected as an autonomous entity, this is the answer of the unconscious psyche."[20]

The "answer of the unconscious psyche" was of course the answer of the entire individuation process and it bore a double relation to the predicament of modernity. Analytical psychology focussed its attention primarily on the affects and images (instincts and archetypes) which undergird the traditional theological doctrines and the attitudes of loyalty which believers bring to them. As such it in effect counseled the withdrawal of projections. While Jung continually insisted throughout his diverse writings on religion that he always returned, insofar as he could, the believing Catholic or Protestant to his traditional faith, this was largely a matter of practical therapeutic strategy. For it is just as clear that his analytical psychology "saw through" the projections of traditional believers. He in effect postulated an archetypal infrastructure--what I would call "the archetype beneath the doctrine"--to traditional belief. Thus, while the good Catholic or Protestant may not know it, his religious faith was motivated by the forces which analytical psychology described. The conceptualization of these forces constituted a system of ideas and a corresponding reality very different from traditional faith. For one to say, "I believe in God the Father," and for one to say, "I am at this moment stirred by an archetype," are two very different explanations of an inner state at a particular moment. In all of this, the thrust of analytical psychology is against traditional Christianity. It is a hermeneutics of suspicion, an unmasking process, a reductive approach, in which dogmas and creeds--the sole modes of conceptualization of traditional faith--are repudiated.

But the withdrawal of projections was only the first of a double movement. Jung believed that he had discovered a natural healing process which occurred when projections were withdrawn--a healing process which would replace, or rather carry forward--the projective process. In the dreams and visions of his patients, especially when they took the form of mandalas, Jung saw a process at work which was remarkably similar to the processes which he believed undergirded the most traditional belief systems. His theory and techniques simply brought this process to a higher level of self-consciousness than they had attained under the conditions of traditional faith. The withdrawal of projections activated new psychological forces, unknown to the traditional believer, which were then raised to a new level of awareness and integrated into self-consciousness. Jung thus ascribed to his own system of ideas a significance functionally equivalent to traditional belief systems. As he put it in an essay written several years earlier:

> It is as though, at the climax of the illness, the destructive powers were converted into healing forces. This is brought about by the archetypes wakening to independent life . . . as a religiously minded person would say: guidance has come from god. With most of my patients I have to avoid this formulation, apt though it is, for it reminds them too much of what they had to reject in the first place. I must express myself in more modest terms and say that the psyche has awakened to spontaneous activity: and indeed this formulation is better suited to the observable facts. . . . To the patient it is nothing less than a revelation. . . .21

Here is Jung's attempt to retrieve meaning from the Christian tradition, his hermeneutics of affirmation.

Situating Jung's Theory of Religion in its Socio-Cultural Context

The question of the extent to which Jung's psychology is Christian and the extent to which it is post-Christian can be further illuminated by situating it more precisely in its socio-cultural context, and in particular, in the context of the phenomenon of modernity. For, at the heart of Jung's thought on religion was his conviction that traditional Christianity and modernity were radically at odds with one another, and he spent much of his life devising a conceptual system which could reconcile the two. In this case we approach Jung's psychology "from the outside" so to speak, whereas the preceding analysis focussed on its internal characteristics. Two theories of modernity, those of Peter Berger and Victor Turner, provide appropriate schema for this task.

Berger's analysis of contemporary life centers upon the process of modernization but especially upon the modernization of consciousness.22 It is the essence of modern consciousness to be irrevocably structured by the technological aspects of industrial production. The individual of today transfers the engineering ethos of modern technology and bureaucracy to his personal consciousness and emotional life. This ethos, characterized by mechanicity, reproducibility and measurability, produces in consciousness the traits of abstraction, functional rationality and instrumentality. Modern consciousness is therefore capable of a degree of self-analysis and self-abstraction never before achieved. As such it is separated from traditional sources of feeling and meaning--it is, in effect, "homeless."

This modernization of consciousness has produced two contrary movements in thought and society. First, it has created an intense nostalgia for the integrative symbols of the past, resulting in a traditionalism which defensively re-affirms ancient symbols of community. Berger calls this movement "counter-modernization." But the modernization of consciousness has also produced an attempt to oppose modernity's emphasis upon the anonymity and abstraction of rationalistic individuality through the creation of new values and a new sense of community which cannot be derived from a sense of tradition.

Berger calls this trend "de-modernization," and finds it best expressed in contemporary youth culture, the counter-culture and the anti-repression psychologies of such writers as Norman O. Brown and R. D. Laing. The principle affirmation of demodernization is the conviction that modern people must re-discover a real and "naked" self which exists beyond institutions and roles--a meta-institutional self--and that the sources for this new self lie in the future creation of fresh and new values. Thus the trend in the direction of demodernization is even more privatized than is the modernization process itself.

Jung's psychology articulates substantially with all three of the trends described by Berger, although in the final analysis I am inclined to place the accent upon the third, demodernization, while nevertheless retaining the other two. Jung's system takes full cognizance of the modernization of consciousness by affirming that modern man must accept the fact that collective ideals and the collective consciousness form the persona, an essential ingredient of his personality. Jung's descriptions of modern man as mass man embody well the principle of functional rationality. The consciousness of modern man was for him truly "homeless." But this state of affairs was also the beginning of the process of individuation. The breakdown of the persona activated the archetypes of the collective unconscious, and called for their assimilation into the ego, thereby broadening the scope of modern man's consciousness and alleviating his condition of homelessness. The archetypes might well be called "structures of tradition." As such their existence and the need for their assimilation constituted the dimension of counter-modernization in Jung's psychology: they are symbols rooted in the ancient past which, when assimilated, unify modern consciousness and overcome its homeless condition.

Jung's psychology did not, however, stop here. He did indeed counsel a return to the past, but only in order that the past might be surpassed. The modern ego must, as it were, pass through the past, on its way to the future. If the individuation process is allowed to continue uninterrupted, the assimilation of the archetypes of the collective unconscious results in the formation of the self, a core of essential, personal uniqueness which exists beyond institutions and roles--in short, a truly "meta-institutional self." As such the self cannot be defined entirely in terms of conformity to either modernity or to tradition; rather, it constitutes a genuinely new structure, composed of more than simply an amalgam of the two. The Jungian self assimilates the past, by means of the archetypes, but it also repudiates the past, for it "sees through" the claims of tradition by penetrating to their archetypal infrastructure. Thus the emergence of the self, the final state of the individuation process, while it is built in part upon modernizing and counter-modernizing processes, also attempts to go beyond these in the direction of demodernization, a view of the person which is entirely new, being neither simply modern nor simply traditional. Jung's psychology is, therefore, an attempt first to codify and then to synthesize all three of these trends as they exist in present-day social and intellectual life, into one unitary system of thought.

Berger's analysis of modernity illumines the question of the status of Jung's view of religion vis-a-vis Christianity, because it permits us to view the double movement of suspicion and affirmation in a sociological perspective. The thrust towards demodernization appears in Jung's psychology in the suspicion and unmasking of traditional Christianity. This is the modern and post-modern facet of Jung's thought. In this sense he is a post-Christian psychologist. But there is also a thrust towards counter-modernization, a move in a backward direction, in order to recover and retrieve something essential from the past. This is Jung's hermeneutics of retrieval, his debt to his Christian heritage. Much of the appeal of Jung's psychology of religion lies in its synthesis of these trends.

There can be little doubt but that Jung's psychology belongs in the most general sense to that genre of thought the overall aim of which is to reflect critically and innovatively upon the problem of modernity and tradition, and that, in consequence of this, his system is best understood in terms of frameworks such as Berger's, addressed as it is precisely to this problem. But it is the purpose of these remarks to situate Jung's psychology in as broad a cultural context as possible, and since Berger's analysis focusses for the most part upon modernity and tradition in the West--although he does draw examples from primitive and non-Western cultures--it is appropriate to explore at least briefly an even broader perspective, that of cultural anthropology.

In point of fact, Jung's psychology submits quite readily to the categories of analysis provided by the anthropologist Victor Turner, in his well-known study, The Ritual Process.23 Such an analysis suggests that Jungian psychology is an expression of massive cultural change, but that the conditions for such change, far from being restricted to the modern period in the West, can be found in other times and other places as well.

Turner's analysis of cultural change is set in the context of what he believes to be two fundamental modalities of human relatedness, which he designates as social structure on the one hand and liminality or communitas on the other hand, although he is almost entirely absorbed by the nature of the latter. Structure refers to the form of social relatedness characterized by heavily institutionalized norms, roles and status positions. These produce an ethos of differentiation and hierarchy, and people view themselves in ways assigned to them by law, custom, convention and ceremonial. From time to time, however, people withdraw from these normal modes of social interaction and enter a structureless or liminal phase in which the customary rules of social organization no longer apply.

This new type of social organization differs point for point from the old. First, the conditions of liminality produce intense comradeship and egalitarianism which involve the whole man in relation to other whole men, creating an overarching sentiment of humankindness. Second, whereas social structure is highly routinized and practical, liminality is charged with affect, immediacy and spontaneity. Third, such social relatedness generates myths, symbols, rituals and philosophical systems. These newly produced systems of imagery and thought serve as a means of reclassifying men's relation to nature, society and culture, as these were conceived under the more orderly conditions of social structure. Finally, the members of communitas together submit to the general authority of ritual elders.

Jung's psychology portrays a form of liminality or communitas. This becomes clear if it is viewed as in essence describing the individuation process, and

39

if that process is considered to be continuous with cultural processes, which include the experiences and principles of psychotherapy, and not simply as a system of ideas. Individuation begins with a withdrawal from normal modes of social action, epitomized by the breakdown of the persona and all that it entails. Such a withdrawal activates the transference relationship, which is accompanied by an intense desire on the part of the patient to be encountered as a whole person. Jung repeatedly counselled a therapeutic attitude characterized by forthrightness and directness, advising his followers to treat their patients as whole persons--otherwise, how were they to become whole themselves? Such attitudes meant eschewing the conventional roles of doctor and physician. The individuation process produced intense spontaneity and affective immediacy, but central to the process as a whole was the creation, at the level of fantasy and mental imagery, of myths, rituals and philosophical systems. Again and again Jung emhasized the potential of the collective unconscious to create, in the form of archetypes, alternative views of reality, views which were necessarily at odds with the ethos of the conventional world from which the patient came. And of course the Jungian therapist serves the function of a ritual elder, a wise man who understands the process of passage from the conventional world, through the unconscious, to that of the new self. He is therefore capable of serving as a guide for those undertaking the experience of individuation. And, as in the case of liminality, much of the imagery of the individuation process consists of the themes of birth and re-birth. It would seem inevitable that such a motif would appear in the mental life of persons who experience themselves as "betwixt and between"--as in transition from one order of reality to another.

But Jung's psychology also departs from Turner's analysis of structure and liminality, and this departure illumines what is its most important and outstanding feature. According to Turner, all liminality must eventually dissolve. It is a state of intensity which cannot exist for very long without some sort of structure to stabilize it. This occurs in one of two ways: either the individual returns to the surrounding social structure--energized to be sure by his own new experiences--or else liminal communities develop their own internal social structure, a condition which Turner calls "normative communitas." However, neither of these alternatives applies to Jung's system nor do they adequately characterize the community of Jungian patients, therapists and teachers. The individuated self of the committed Jungian returns to the social order only in an extremely instrumental manner, and the social organization of the Jungian community is very loose and unstructured, although there is some hierarchy in the contrasting positions of, say, lay Jungian as opposed to a supervising analyst. For these reasons it is more correct to say that Jung's psychology presents the student of cultural change with a form of "permanent liminality" in which there is no need to return to social structure, or to generate a social structure internal to the community. Instead, the individuated person simply continues to interpret himself and the world about him in terms of Jungian categories. In point of fact, for the Jungian--be he patient, therapist or teacher--the problem of social order ceases to exist at all: it has been replaced by the problem of inner, psychological order.

Turner's analysis of structure and liminality provides a broad, cultural perspective upon the nature of Jung's psychology as a whole, and especially his psychological theory of religion. Social structure, as Turner conceives it, appears in Jung's thought as an individual's conformity to the doctrines of traditional Christianity, which is accompanied by an uncritical and unreflective adaptation to the institutions of the social order--in this instance, the institution of the traditional church. Hence Jung's hermeneutic of suspicion, the first of his two-fold movement, is, from Turner's perspective, a critical move against social structure. On the other hand, the second phase of Jung's double movement consists of the emergence of the individuation process, in which the individual turns away from the dogmas of traditional Christianity, in other words, away from structure, and directs his attention to the inner workings of the self, which engages the images of genuine religious experience. These images lie beneath, so to speak, beliefs and dogma. This second move, which is Jung's attempt to retrieve meaning from traditional Christianity, can be understood as a move towards liminality and all that it suggests. Only under the conditions of liminality is genuine religion possible for Jung.

This shift of the locus of meaning and order from

the social and traditional to the inner, personal, psychological sphere is the central conceptual leit-motif running throughout both Jung's psychology and his theory of religion. The fact that his psychology of religion so richly structures the inner diffuseness which accompanies suspicion of the social order and of traditional religion is his greatest achievement. But the fact that his thought eschews the social order and the possibility that religion might organize that order is also a major limitation. Jung did not see the pervasiveness--so convincingly emphasized by current social science--of the institutional organization of the private sector. Thus, the final assessment of Jung's work must remain a double one.

NOTES

1. C. G. Jung, _Two Essays on Analytical Psychology_, trans. R. F. C. Hull, _Collected Works_, Vol. 7 (New York: Pantheon Books, Inc., 1966).

2. Paul Ricoeur, _Freud and Philosophy_, trans. Denis Savage, (New Haven: Yale University Press, 1970).

3. D. Cox, _Jung and St. Paul_ (New York: Association Press, 1959).

4. H. Schaer, _Religion and the Cure of Souls in Jung's Psychology_ (New York: Pantheon Books, Inc., 1950).

5. V. White, _God and the Unconscious_ (Cleveland: The World Publishing Company, 1952).

6. R. Hostie, _Religion and the Psychology of C. G. Jung_ (New York: Sheed and Ward, 1957).

7. H. L. Philip, _Jung and the Problem of Evil_ (London: Rockliff, 1958).

8. P. Rieff, _The Triumph of the Therapeutic_ (New York: Harper and Row, 1966).

9. W. A. Johnson, _The Search for Transcendence_ (New York: Harper and Row, 1974).

10. C. G. Jung, _Two Essays on Analytical Psychology_, p. 229.

11. _Ibid._, p. 235.

12. _Ibid._, p. 238.

13. C. G. Jung, _Psychology and Religion_, trans. R. F. C. Hull, _Collected Works_, Vol. 11 (New York: Pantheon Books, Inc., 1963), pp. 3-106.

14. _Ibid._, p. 8.

15. _Ibid._, p. 9.

16. Ibid., p. 81.

17. Ibid., p. 82.

18. Ibid., p. 83, 87.

19. Ibid., p. 95.

20. Ibid., p. 96.

21. C. G. Jung, "Psychotherapists or Clergy," *Collected Works*, Vol. 11, p. 345.

22. Peter Berger, *The Homeless Mind*, with B. Berger and H. Kellner (New York: Random House, 1973).

23. Victor Turner, *The Ritual Process* (Chicago: Aldine Publishing Company, 1969).

CHAPTER 3

JUNG AND THE PHENOMENOLOGY OF RELIGION

William E. Paden

> Phenomenology . . . is not a method
> that has been reflectively elaborated, but
> is man's true vital activity, consisting in
> losing himself neither in things nor in the
> ego, neither in hovering above objects like
> a god nor dealing with them like an animal,
> but in doing what is given to neither animal
> nor god: standing aside and understanding
> what appears into view.
> --Gerardus van der Leeuwl

The psychological elucidation of these
images, which cannot be passed over in
silence or blindly ignored, leads logically
into the depths of religious phenomenology.
The history of religion in its widest sense
(including therefore mythology, folklore,
and primitive psychology) is a
treasure-house of archetypal forms from
which the doctor can draw helpful parallels
and enlightening comparisons for the purpose
of calming and clarifying a consciousness
that is all at sea. It is absolutely
necessary to supply these fantastic images
that rise up so strange and threatening
before the mind's eye with some kind of
context so as to make them more
intelligible. Experience has shown that the
best way to do this is by means of
comparative mythological material.

45

This paper examines and assesses the relationship between Jung's work and that aspect of religious studies known as the phenomenology of religion.3 The latter presents a certain claim to be the systematic, as distinguished from the historical, study of religion. While it can mean something as broad as the "objective" rather than sectarian approach to religious facts, it is more specifically identified with the comparative, morphological approach of figures like Gerardus van der Leeuw and Mircea Eliade. As religion now becomes a secular subject matter, the methodological foundations of phenomenology of religion's legacy must draw closer scrutiny.4

At the same time, while much has been written about Jung and religion, little has been said about Jung and the study of religion.5 While Jung's concepts developed for the most part independently of the academic field of religion, there is much in them that is similar in method and that provides mutually illuminating comparison. This study outlines a context for reading Jung's work in relation to religious phenomenology, focusing on his method rather than content.

Certainly during the formative period of Jung's career, 1900-1920, the phenomenology of religion was an inconspicuous intellectual force, primarily located in the Netherlands and Scandinavia, and had nothing of the popularity it drew after the publication of van der Leeuw's _Phaenomenologie der Religion_ in 1933. Jung was in any case influenced more by the turn of the century search for universal structures and the psychoanalytic circle's attempts then to open up the realm of mythology to psychological understanding. As in James G. Frazer's work at that time, religion was just one of many sources from which the new anthropologies and psychologies could draw in reconstructing the history of human consciousness, and it was with the triumph of these human sciences that religion became no longer the assumed filter for viewing history, but itself a datum to be viewed and interpreted.

Jung uses the term "phenomenology"6 often and in

different contexts. The following analysis identifies and describes these, and shows how they compare with types of phenomenological perspective found in religious studies, namely, 1) the bracketing of judgment (the "epoche"), 2) acknowledgement of the dimension of the "numinous," 3) morphology, 4) hermeneutics, 5) the analysis of archetypal structures.

One issue immediately intrudes into such discussion and might even appear to challenge its validity: the uneasy embeddedness of Jung's phenomenological references within a larger system of theory and explanation. Jung had to explain and protect his view of the psyche with a repertoire of conceptual frameworks, and Kantianism, Platonism, instinct-theory, empiricism, and phenomenology were the multiple ways he gave context to his findings. In this process, Jung's "phenomenology" became bedfellow with altogether different kinds of approaches. But this oscillation is comprehended and appreciated better through careful study of the phenomenological components in his work.

Bracketing

The first condition of any phenomenological approach to religion is adherence to the double-edged axiom of the primacy of observation and suspension of the attempt to do metaphysics. This step is necessary so that description and understanding will derive from the phenomenon and its own presented world rather than from presuppositions or biases about it derived from the interpreter's world. In a time and field dominated by theology, metaphysics, and evolutionism, the objective study of religion was made possible only by this wedge which allowed religious facts to become subjects for investigation and not pawns to prove existing theories. While a certain objective—as opposed to sectarian—attitude definitely emerged in the mid-nineteenth century in correlation with the notion of a "science of religion," it was only after the turn of the century that the specific Husserlian concept of the epoche was appropriated by religionists.7 Today religion scholars vary in how they interpret this "bracketing": for some it means neutrality and linkage with science, for others a preparatory or ancillary discipline for the higher enterprise of revealed theology, and for still others an engagement with the life of the subject matter.

47

Jung's writings are permeated with this fundamental definition of phenomenology as a descriptive rather than metaphysical affair. He is explicit and tireless in stating that his work did not tred beyond the observable. "Although I have often been called a philosopher," he writes, "I am an empiricist and adhere as such to the phenomenological standpoint."8 More fully, he states that the methodological approach of his psychology is

> exclusively phenomenological, that is, it is concerned with occurrences, events, experiences--in a word, with facts. Its truth is a fact and not a judgment. When psychology speaks, for instance, of the motif of the virgin birth, it is only concerned with the fact that there is such an idea, but it is not concerned with the question whether such an idea is true or false in any other sense . . .

> This point of view is the same as that of natural science. Psychology deals with ideas and other mental contents as zoology, for instance, deals with the different species of animals. An elephant is "true" because it exists. The elephant is neither an inference nor a statement nor the subjective judgment of a creator. It is a phenomenon. But we are so used to the idea that psychic events are wilful and arbitrary products, or even the inventions of a human creator, that we can hardly rid ourselves of the prejudiced view that the psyche and its contents are nothing but our own arbitrary invention or the more or less illusory product of supposition and judgment.9

Jung clearly saw himself as working the middle territory between theologians and "reductionistic" scientists, and as "neither hovering above objects like a god nor dealing with them like an animal." He therefore had to defend his method on both fronts, assuring one group that he was not taking any "otherness" away from religious experience, and the other that he was taking true scientific investigation seriously. "No metaphysical assertions will be found in my writings," he writes in a letter, "and n.b., no denials of metaphysical assertions."10 Disdaining the presumptuousness of both "know it all" metaphysians and "know it all" reductionists, Jung insisted upon, carved out, and extended this in-between, descriptive space. Within that space, any experience, no matter how mystical, private, oneiric, or culturally sacrosanct, becomes a phenomenon for study. On this ground alone, Jung offers a major connection with religious phenomenology.

"Phenomenology" here means just what its etymology says, the study of that which appears, and it is distinguished from explanations which speak of what things "are" in themselves or in their ultimate, transcendental nature. Jung tied psychology to phenomenology by maintaining that "psyche is the only phenomenon that is given to us immediately."[11] It follows that "archetypes" cannot be verified scientifically, that their objective existence is "unrepresentable," and that only their "effects" can be seen and compared. Gods, as instances of archetypes, are in the same kind of category: knowable only in appearance, image, experience. Jung likened this viewpoint to paradigms in physics, where the smallest particles

> are themselves irrepresentable but have effects from the nature of which we can build up a model. The archetypal image, the motif or mythologem, is a construction of this kind.[12]

From this passage we can see that Jung was not entirely opposed to explanations. It was their interference with observation that he eschewed:

> In view of the enormous complexity of psychic phenomena, a purely phenomenological point of view is, and will be for a long time, the only possible one and the only one with any prospect of success. "Whence" things come and "what" they are, these, particularly in the field of psychology, are questions which are apt to call forth untimely attempts at explanation.[13]

Although van der Leeuw as theologian and Jung as scientist approached the middle ground of phenomenology from opposite sides of the courtyard, there is strikingly little difference between their concepts of bracketing. For both, the study of appearances meant that one must stick to human experience (of the sacred, in this case) and not cross over from that experience to questions of what lies ultimately or "objectively" behind it. But when Jung noted that "we can do no more than carefully tap out the phenomenology that gives us indirect news of the essence of the psyche,"14 he was saying that appearances are indeed pointers to that which they are appearances of. And similarly, while van der Leeuw had begun his famous work by asserting that phenomenology deals only "with the activity of man in his relation to God," and that "of the acts of God Himself" it "can give no account whatever,"15 he did conclude that

> To see face to face is denied us. But much can be observed even in a mirror; and it is possible to speak about things seen.16

Jung did acknowledge a Jamesian line between science and personal "over-beliefs." Of the boundary, the psychology of religious experience, he wrote in a letter:

> We come here to the "frontier of the human," of which G. van Le Fort says that it is the "portcullis of God." In my private capacity as a man I can only concur with this view, but with the best will in the world I cannot maintain that this is a verifiable assertion, which is what science is all about in the end. It is a subjective confession which has no place in science.17

Phenomenology of the Numinous

A second facet of the phenomenological approach to religion involves acknowledging and identifying the unique characteristics of religious experience. From the anthropological interest in "mana" at the turn of the century, through Otto's The Idea of the Holy and Eliade's wide-ranging use of the concept of "the sacred," all religious phenomenology has revolved around the notion that homo religiosus is he whose world is defined in terms of the experience of an "other" power that intersects with and defines his life.

On the surface Jung presented his work as

50

continuous with this tradition by regularly using the term "numinous" to describe the ego's experience of the "otherness" or overwhelming autonomy of unconscious symbols and contents. His Terry Lectures concisely defined this stance:

> In speaking of religion I must make clear from the start what I mean by that term. Religion, as the Latin word denotes, is a careful and scrupulous observation of what Rudolf Otto aptly termed the numinosum, that is, a dynamic agency or effect not caused by an arbitrary act of will. On the contrary, it seizes and controls the human subject, who is always rather its victim than its creator. The numinosum--whatever its cause may be--is an experience of the subject independent of his will.18

Jung also accepted "mana" as the fundamental archetype from which God-images were formed.19

At the same time, "numinous," "numen," and "numinosity" appear in Jung's writings not to show the sui generis character of religious as opposed to "natural" experience, but to describe the facts and phenomenology of the unconscious and its archetypes by showing their religious or "god-like" aspect. Just as for Otto the term "numinous" perfectly expressed the opus proprium et alienum of the "God of Abraham, Isaac, and Jacob," so for Jung it accurately expressed the ecstatic relationship of ego to the involuntary, uncontrollable, and possessive aspects of unconscious archetypes.

Jung's idea of the numinous therefore operated within a strictly experiential, phenomenological framework that acknowledged the way ego is invaded by non-ego. This approach, unlike Otto's, did not require an objectivistic, Neo-Kantian or Biblical context. It did account for the experience of that which independently confronts and challenges consciousness. "Even the soberest formulation of the phenomenology of complexes," he wrote, "cannot get around the impressive fact of their autonomy."20 Archetypes take expression in gods, spirits, and daemonic agencies, have a will and presence of their own, and overwhelm the individual. This is the basis of spiritual or mystical experience21 and the ecstatic moments of psychic openness that accompany the individuation process,22 as well as the "terrifying suggestibility that lies behind all psychic mass movements."23

In these ways Jung's approach accommodates religious experience of the "Other," "Thou," or "God." Without making claims about what these "are" outside of our experience of them, his psychology acknowledges their reality and presence as counterpositions to the subjective ego.24

Between Morphology and Hermeneutics

A third component of phenomenology involves analysis and interpretation of forms, types and structures of religious life. The first, cataloguing stage of this activity was set forth in 1887 in P. D. Chantepie de la Saussaye's *Lehrbuch der Religionsgeschichte*,25 an encyclopedia of religion which divided its contents into "Historical" and "Phenomenological" sections. In the latter Chantepie presented an inventory of all types of religious life, e.g., sacred space, sacrifice, festivals, priesthood, and above all, various kinds of objects of worship, from stones to monotheism. While religious morphologies had existed before Chantepie,26 it was the function of this work to establish religion as a legitimate subject matter for academic investigation by showing that it was data that could not only be collected but also organized and analyzed along objective lines.

But with figures like van der Leeuw and Eliade this inventorial approach gave way to a second kind of interest in forms, one that was not concerned with collecting but with interpreting. The emphasis of Eliade's *Patterns in Comparative Religion*27 was not on the existence of types, but their meaning and functions as religious expressions. The study of a pattern, like New Year's rites or the mythic valorization of the sky, became a resource and tool for interpreting particular instances and innovations of that pattern, so that the comparativist could go back and forth between the type and the particular, the genus and the species, the archetypal and the historical. The phenomenological element in this was the process of "saving" appearances from merely historical, causal contexts of explanation, by investigating their meaning as structures of the experience of the sacred.

52

Jung's work paralleled both of these activities. Jung the scientist liked to tell potential critics that the classification of what appeared in experience under certain definite types was a method of natural science "applied wherever we have to do with multifarious and still unorganized material."28 Thus archetypes are not theoretical inventions and not mythology, but "purely empirical" concepts, whose "sole purpose is to give a name to a group of related or analogous psychic phenomena."29 The concept "anima," for example, "does no more and means no more than, shall we say, the concept 'arthropods' which includes all animals with articulated body and limbs and so gives a name to this phenomenological group."30 Such statements seem to bespeak the tabular world of Linnaeus. In the following longer quote Jung presents himself as such a cataloguer:

> Since for years I have been observing and investigating the products of the unconscious in the widest sense of the word, namely dreams, fantasies, visions, and delusions of the insane, I have not been able to avoid recognizing certain regularities, that is, types. There are types of situations and types of figures that repeat themselves frequently and have a corresponding meaning. I therefore employ the term "motif" to designate these repetitions. Thus there are not only typical dreams but typical motifs in the dreams. These may, as we have said, be situations or figures. Among the latter there are human figures that can be arranged under a series of archetypes, the chief of them being, according to my suggestion, the shadow, the wise old man, the child (including the child hero), the mother ("Primordial Mother" and "Earth Mother") as a supraordinate personality . . . and her counterpart, the maiden, and lastly the anima in man and the animus in woman.31

His closing comment contains an almost facetious tone: "The above types are far from exhausting all the statistical regularities in this respect."32

But Jung's work clearly was not limited to the static classification of symbols. More importantly his "phenomenology" also became a method of interpretation, a way to unfold the intelligibility of individual phenomena by supplying their comparative or collective context. His move toward the comparative method as an exegetical tool was prompted by a combination of personal, historical, scientific and clinical circumstances, a play of contexts and vectors that had the effect of making his work inscrutable to many. First, at the most basic level, comparative perspective was a personal necessity:

> . . . I had to find evidence for the historical prefiguration of my inner experiences. That is to say, I had to ask myself, "Where have my particular premises already occurred in history?"33

Secondly, the comparative method came from the life of Jung the therapist, drawing on mythological parallels for the purpose of interpreting the extraordinary symbolic universes of his patients. Third, it was an approach required for scientific understanding:

> The psychologist must depend in the highest degree upon historical and literary parallels if he wishes to exclude at least the crudest errors of judgment.34

And finally, Jung was motivated to push beyond Freud's "reductive personalism" and singular interpretation of the Oedipus Myth metaphor to seek out a larger, transpersonal basis for the theory of the unconscious. While "Freud's method," he wrote, "consisted in the application of an already existing theory, my method was a comparative one."35 The jungle-like 500 page exegesis of "Miss Miller's" fantasies (Symbols of Transformation, 1912) with its myriad "parallels" from exotic sources, revealed neither the cataloguing manner of an old world botanist, nor the methodical style of a thematic literature search. It represented both personal and professional quests for a transpersonal perspective on the psyche, for higher hermeneutical ground.

In some contexts Jung used the term "phenomenology" to mean the study of what is general, typical or thematic in experience. Without knowledge of a "general phenomenology" of the psyche, he stated, psychologies like Freud's are "left hanging in mid air."36 He added that

. . . in each individual case that we observe scientifically, we have to consider the manifestations of the psyche in their totality. . . . if we want to understand the psyche, we have to include the whole world.37

Therefore, the psychologist cannot be limited to the serialized study of individual cases, or to corraling them into one mythology, but must discern and understand general patterns and thereby bring thematic context to otherwise singular, disconnected phenomena:

The more complex the phenomena which we have to do with in practical treatment, the wider must be our frame of reference and the greater the corresponding knowledge.

Anyone, therefore, who does not know the universal distribution and significance of the syzygy motif in the psychology of primitives, in mythology, in comparative religion, and in the history of literature, can hardly claim to say anything about the concept of the anima. His knowledge of the psychology of the neurosis may give him some idea of it, but it is only a knowledge of its general phenomenology that could open his eyes to the real meaning of what he encounters in individual cases, often in pathologically distorted form.38

In his 1928 lecture, "A Psychological Theory of Types," Jung has used the term "phenomenology" in a similar way:

My more limited field of work is not the clinical study of external characteristics, but the investigation and classification of the psychic data which may be inferred from them. The first result of this work is a phenomenology of the psyche, which enables us to formulate a corresponding theory about its structure...

Clinical studies are based on the description of symptoms, and the step from this to a phenomenology of the psyche is comparable to the step from a purely

55

symptomatic pathology to the pathology of cellular and metabolic processes. This is to say, the phenomenology of the psyche brings into view these psychic processes in the background which underlie the clinical symptoms.39

The above quotations present phenomenology as that which describes the generic context of individual experiences, experiences whose meanings are not initially given and that require an understanding of their own "background" in order to appear as what they really are.40

Jung's comparative method was a two-way street, with cognitive and therapeutic sides. On the one hand he expanded his sense of the "general" phenomenology of a symbol through encounters with its many versions, and on the other he expanded his and his patients' sense of a particular problem by reference to its collective parallels, parallels that yielded "priceless" analogies. The latter process he called the "hermeneutic method"41 or "constructive method,"42 and Symbols of Transformation epitomized it. The procedure was not derived from the requirements of an objective science, but from the challenge of understanding the intentionality--as distinguished from the simple components--of a patient's life process. Here "constructive" was opposed to "reductive" or "causal" methods, and meant building up a sense of an individual's "context" through analogues (e.g., from mythology) that would bring out the telos or direction of that situation, as opposed to analytically "breaking down" a life into backward-looking parts.43 Jung's early experience of deciphering the purposive rather than the literal or objective meaning of schizophrenic patients' behavior and language lay behind this concern--the bizarre and insane at the Burghoelzli Clinic symptomized worlds that could in this way become intelligible and not dismissed as the products of diseased brain cells gone amuck.

The "hermeneutic" method therefore assumes that symbols are not just veils for known instincts, but attempts "to elucidate, by means of analogy, something that still belongs entirely to the domain of the unknown or something that is yet to be."44 He adds:

The essential character of

hermeneutics, a science which was widely practised in former times, consists in making successive additions of other analogies to the analogy given in the symbol: in the first place of subjective analogies produced at random by the patient, and then of objective analogies found by the analyst in the course of erudite research. This procedure widens and enriches the initial symbol, and the final outcome is an infinitely complex and varied picture, in which certain "lines" of psychological development stand out as possibilities that are at once individual and collective. There is no science on earth by which these lines could be proved "right": on the contrary, rationalism could very easily prove that they are not right. Their validity is proved by their intense value for life. And that is what matters from the point of view of practical treatment. The important thing is that men should have life, not that the principles by which they live should be demonstrable rationally as "right."45

Jung had recognized early on (1914) that while this method could lead to the possibility of scientific theory, it would be "superstition" to consider it science in itself.46

Jung's exegesis of the "Miss Miller" material bears a striking comparison to what Frazer attempted in The Golden Bough (first published in 1890). Each began with an "unknown" phenomenon, and sought its explanation by resort to the comparative method of marshalling parallels. The archaic Roman rite of priesthood succession and the fantasies of a modern educated American woman were thus given a thematic context geared to illumine the original data by uncovering their universal structures. Jung admired Frazer's work as "a splendid example" of the "composite method" of understanding primitive psychology by drawing on a variety of resources.47 But the differences are equally interesting: Frazer the rationalist performed the autopsy of a cultural corpse, while Jung the romantic attended the reincarnation of the gods.

The "general phenomenology" of Jung, in which

symbol and archetype amplify each other's meaning, bears closer resemblance to the modern project of Eliade, whose study of the "transhistorical" structure of symbols parallels Jung's interest in their "transpersonal" character.48   For both, comparative knowledge and process is used to exegete what might be called respectively the texts of culture and psyche. Against their proper archetypal background, a Balinese "navel of the world" temple and a Burghoelzli inmate's dream can receive structural elucidation. At the 1950 Eranos Conference, Eliade even spoke of the religionist doing for culture what depth psychology was doing for individuals:

> We have dared to use the term metapsychoanalysis because what is in question here is a more spiritual technique, applicable mainly to elucidating the theoretical content of the symbols and archetypes, giving transparency and coherence to what is allusive, cryptic or fragmentary.49

Through such comparative perspective Jung as hermeneut tried to rescue psyche from the density and particularity of ego constructs, while Eliade pursues the rescue of modern culture from its historicism. And as the shadow, anima and Self archetypes were arrived at by observing many patients, and in turn became concepts used to deepen an understanding of particular patients, so sacred space, time and nature were for Eliade arrived at by observing many cultures, and in turn became concepts used to interpret particular cultures.

Phenomenology of Symbols

At various times Jung refers to the "phenomenology" of a symbol or archetype as though it had unique, defining motifs and structures that characterized it and could be elucidated. Hence he speaks of the "special phenomenology of the child archetype," "the phenomenology of the spirit in fairytales," or, as in the subtitle of the book, Aion, "researches into the phenomenology of the self." This more particular use of the term seems to parallel the religionist's concepts of the "phenomenology" of particular forms like sacrifice, initiation, or cosmogonies.

His account of the child archetype is a case in point. Jung identifies specific motifs typifying it: abandonment, invincibility, hermaphroditism, and the child as representing "beginning and end." The "child" means something "evolving toward independence" and "this it cannot do without detaching itself from its origins: abandonment is therefore a necessary condition, not just a concomitant symptom."50 He writes:

> Abandonment, exposure, danger, etc., are all elaborations of the "child's" insignificant beginning and of its mysterious and miraculous birth. This statement describes a certain psychic experience of a creative nature, whose object is the emergence of a new and as yet unknown content.51

The invincibility of the child:

> represents the strongest, the most ineluctable urge in every being, namely the urge to realize itself. It is, as it were, an incarnation of the inability to do otherwise, equipped with all the powers of nature and instinct . . .52

This specific method of deciphering the essential form of a symbol behind its particular contents is similar to Eliades' treatment of "patterns," such as stones:

> The hardness, ruggedness, and permanence of matter was in itself a hierophany in the religious consciousness of the primitive. And nothing was more direct and autonomous in the completeness of its strength, nothing more noble or more awe-inspiring, than majestic rock . . . Above all, stone is. It always remains itself, and exists of itself . . . man finds in it an obstacle--if not to his body, at least to his gaze . . . Rock shows him something that transcends the precariousness of his humanity: an absolute mode of being . . . In its grandeur, its hardness, its shape, and its colour, man is faced with a reality and a force that belong to some world other than the profane world of which he is himself a part.53

And yet, while the Child, the Mother and the Trickster each __have__ a specific phenomenology in terms of experiential patterns, it is clear that archetypes in their "unprojected" state do not have a determined meaning. Jung admits that

> This seems to contradict the concept of a "type." If I am not mistaken, it not only seems but actually __is__ a contradiction. Empirically speaking, we are dealing all the time with "types," definite forms that can be named and distinguished. But as soon as you divest these types of the phenomenology presented by the case material, and try to examine them in relation to other archetypal forms, they branch out into such far-reaching ramifications in the history of symbols that one comes to the conclusion that the basic psychic elements are infinitely varied and ever changing, so as utterly to defy our powers of imagination.54

Jung therefore resisted--not always successfully--"objective" accounts of archetypes because he believed that we only glimpse their meaning in the lives and situations of individuals.55 In itself a symbol's reference is limitless and consequently there can be no unilateral or clear-cut formulation of its meaning.

In this regard, Marie-Louise von Franz cautions against those who write about archetypes but who "do not take as a starting point the human individual and his psychic structure," and who "sit in the middle of the archetype, so to speak, and let it amplify itself, poetically and 'scientifically'."56 She adds:

> As soon as one approaches an archetype in this way, everything becomes everything. If you start with the world tree, you can easily prove that every mythological motif leads to the world tree in the end. If you start with the sun, you can easily prove that everything is the sun . . . And so you just get lost in the chaos of interconnections and overlappings of meanings which all archetypal images have with one another . . . you can pile up comparative material forever, but you have completely lost your Archimedean standpoint

from which to interpret.57

Conclusions

The above strands of Jung's "phenomenology" form
a direct parallel in emphasis and scope with their
counterparts in the study of religion. The similarity
between them is seen most fundamentally in the
methodical respect for experience and the need for
"comparative" understanding.

While Jung limited his archetypal interests to
themes representing certain individuation processes,
he succeeded in bringing mainstream Western religious
symbols clearly into a framework for phenomenological
study. For one who worked outside the
Religionswissenschaft tradition, this was a remarkable
intellectual accomplishment, and contrasts revealingly
with the work of more pedigreed comparative
religionists who took only non-Western universes for
their field of observation, thus leaving the
Judeo-Christian material to theologians and
philosophers. It does not detract from this
contribution that Jung himself was fascinated less by
faith, hope and charity than by syzygies, mandalas and
quaternities.

Nor does the fact that Jung saw religious
phenomena as expressions of the unconscious rather
than as manifestations of "the Sacred" detract from
the phenomenological force of his work. If anything,
orthodox religionists have for decades used a covertly
theological framework for their descriptive
morphologies, in which the "sacred" becomes in effect
a neutral term for God or the divine. This
supernatural power is then seen to be "manifest"--one
thinks of the old "from idolatry to monotheism"
schemas--in various kinds of objects, e.g., water,
stones, sky, space, ancestors, rites, gods. The
result is a natural theology in phenomenological
guise: an arraying of the many ways through which the
transcendent is experienced by man. Jung's
psychological framework, however, while also giving
centrality to the experience of "the other," and thus
encompassing religious experience, does not present
alterity as only revealing or refracting itself
through so many objects and forms, but focuses on the
varied but dialectical relationships of ego and
non-ego, subject and object.

61

Jung's comparative work was neither carried out by the social-scientific method of careful and controlled cross-cultural observation, nor by a philosophia perennis vision apprehending East and West together in universal perspective. The comparative vector in Jung is not found in assertions that "all cultures say the same thing," or that "there are lots of Saviors, therefore Jesus is not absolute," or even that "the Goddess is the same everywhere." It is rather seen in his need to ground individual experience in its thematic context and thus to understand it, clarify it, and extricate it from inchoate isolation. In this, Jung's scientific and morphological concerns joined with his "constructive method" and mission as a therapist and hermeneut. Was his phenomenology a scientific anatomy, or was it essentially wise advice to Miss Miller? It was both, and one aspect could not exist without the other.

Jung rarely stopped to distinguish between the scientific and hermeneutical poles that his term "phenomenology" embraced. Back and forth he went between demonstrating archetypal structures and engaging in creative "amplification." Because phenomenologists of religion undergo similar oscillations, Jungians and religionists alike could use more clarification of their comparative methods, and could benefit from clearer distinctions between interpreting the "living" symbolism of a myth on the one hand, and making cross-cultural generalizations about myth on the other.

If Jung's psychological framework is in some ways a phenomenological asset for or extension of religious studies, by the systematic omission of "social man" it also perpetuates a blind spot. Religious life, after all, is not only an inward matter, but also a response to something outwardly and uniquely "given" by external culture and community. That dreams were Jung's main source of material for demonstrating archetypes, and that in spite of his notion of the "collective" he indicates no real grasp of Durkheimian theory,58 shows how utterly peripheral is this externality of man's social life and the reality of "communitas." Peter Homans rightly notes here the "devaluation" of social structure "in the interests of a private self," and Jung's tendency to view "the social order as destructive of personal, inner, integrity rather than as a means of fulfilling and completing that integrity."59

62

Nor is this exclusion Jung's alone. Phenomenologists of religion have also portrayed the sacred in serene disregard of its social contexts and intentionalities, hoping thereby to preserve and testify to its _sui generis_ character. That both the content and the structure of religious life are typically generated by the desire to embody or act out what is sacred for one's particular community should pose no methodological threat. But this social, ethical, relational space, with its myriad variations and virtuosi, and abundance of archetypal material,60 has had no place, yet, in the more cosmic and hermetic Jungian and Eliadean universes. There remains an underdeveloped understanding of the external, cultural, and collective structuring of what is actually sacred among actual people.

The phenomenology of religion—still an unsettled phrase with an uncertain future—never has been free from specific thematic agendas, or from the hermeneutical needs of its culture and individual exponents. In its first phase, responding to the chaos of data, it produced inventories, maps, and classifications. Later it faced metaphysical establishments and advocated the primacy of data to judgment. It faced the problems of "objectification" and reductionism and in response developed the ideal of Verstehen and the close observation of lived experience. To supplement and balance the historical approach, it asserted through van der Leeuw and Eliade the necessity of the comparative perspective. Amidst these configurations of the phenomenology of religion, Jung's work, with its paradoxical equation of phenomenology and psychology, extends, mirrors, and challenges its religious analogues.

1. Religion in Essence and Manifestation, trans. J. E. Turner (New York: Harper and Row, 1963), Vol. II, p. 676.

2. The Collected Works of C. G. Jung, ed. by Herbert Read, et. al., Vol. 12, trans. R. F. C. Hull (Princeton: Princeton University Press, 1970), 2nd edition, p. 33. Subsequent references to the Collected Works will be noted as CW, followed by volume and page number.

3. For general reviews of the "phenomenology of religion" see Åke Hultkrantz, "The Phenomenology of Religion: Aims and Methods," Temenos, VI (1970), pp. 68-88; Eric C. Sharpe, Comparative Religion: A History (London: Duckworth, 1975), Chapter Ten; and Jacques Waardenburg, "Religion Between Reality and Idea: A Century of Phenomenology of Religion in the Netherlands," Numen, XIX (August, 1972), pp. 128-203. A current review, assessment and bibliography of the phenomenology of religion discipline since World War II is Ursula King's "Historical and Phenomenological Approaches to the Study of Religion," in Contemporary Approaches to the Study of Religion, Vol. I: the Humanities, Religion and Reason Series 27, ed. by Frank Whaling, pp. 29-164 (Berlin: de Gruyter, 1984).

4. For a critique of religious phenomenology see Hans H. Penner, "Is Phenomenology a Method for the Study of Religion?," Bucknell Review, XXXVII, (Spring, 1970), pp. 29-54. Penner's gauntlet has scarcely been taken up. See also his critique of the encyclopedia, Historia Religionum (Leiden: Brill, 1969, 1971) in "The Fall and Rise of Methodology: A Retrospective Review," Religious Studies Review, Vol. II, No. 1 (January, 1976), pp. 11-16. Jacques Waardenburg's Reflections on the Study of Religion, Religion and Reason Series 15 (The Hague: Mouton, 1978), urges a distinction between "classical" and "new style" phenomenology. Where the former dealt with objective patterns, the latter will attempt to understand the actual intentions and specific,

spiritual universes of religious people. The recent work by Walter L. Brenneman, Jr., Stanley O. Yarian and Alan M. Olson, The Seeing Eye: Hermeneutical Phenomenology in the Study of Religion (University Park, Pa.: Pennsylvania State University Press, 1982) attempts to define religious phenomenology in terms of a self-reflective engagement with "the other," and thus makes a definite departure from the typological approach of Continental Religionswissenschaft.

5. James W. Heisig's Imago Dei: A Study of C. G. Jung's Psychology of Religion (Lewisburg: Bucknell University Press, 1979) is a useful research tool.

6. As Heisig and Spiegelberg both note, Jung never attempted to identify with continental philosophical phenomenology, i.e., the movement begun by Brentano and Husserl. There is not a single reference to them in the Collected Works. Cf. Heisig, p. 195, fn. 27, for some interpretations of Jung's relation to philosophical phenomenology, and also Herbert Spiegelberg, Phenomenology in Psychology and Psychiatry: An Historical Introduction (Evanston, Illinois: Northwestern University Press, 1972), pp. 130-131. At no point in his writings does Jung engage in methodological discussion with the Swiss leaders of phenomenological psychiatry, Ludwig Binswanger (1881-1966) and Medard Boss (1903-   ). Finally, Jung never refers to the "phenomenology of religion" per se, i.e., as an academic discipline. The closest he comes is in noting the need for psychologists to have an "accurate knowledge of the phenomenology of religious experience, which is a subject in itself" (CW, 9, i, 62). Jung's Symbols of Transformation (1912) does refer to the 1905 edition of Chantepie de la Saussaye's Lehrbuch der Religionsgeschichte, but ironically Chantepie had taken his famous "phenomenological section" out of this printing in order to work out its philosophical underpinnings. Cf. Sharpe, p. 223.

7. It is notable, though, that in spite of the borrowing of this term (from the Greek verb, epecho, "I hold back," referring to the act of

65

stopping or bracketing metaphysical judgments) the phenomenology of religion as a subdivision of European Religionswissenschaft is a completely independent tradition from that of Husserl, with its genealogy going back to 18th and 19th century attempts at morphologies of religion.

8. CW, 11, p. 5.

9. Ibid., pp. 6-7.

10. C. G. Jung Letters, ed. Gerhard Adler, trans. R. F. C. Hull (Princeton: Princeton University Press, 1973), Vol. I, p. 557.

11. CW, 8, p. 139.

12. Ibid., p. 215.

13. CW, 9, Part One, p. 182.

14. C. G. Jung Letters, p. 546.

15. Gerardus van der Leeuw, Religion in Essence and Manifestation, p. 23.

16. Ibid., p. 678.

17. C. G. Jung Letters, op. cit., p. 556.

18. CW, 11, p. 7.

19. For example, see CW, 7, pp. 67-68.

20. CW, 8, p. 97.

21. Ibid., p. 186.

22. CW, 11, p. 294.

23. Ibid., p. 184.

24. Jung explains this forcefully in reply to Martin Buber's accusations about metaphysical presumption and "gnosticism." See "Religion and Psychology: A Reply to Martin Buber," CW, 18, pp. 663-670.

25. Published in English as Manual of the Science of Religion, trans. Beatrice S. Colyer-Fergusson

(London: Longmans, Green and Company, 1891).

26. For an analysis of the history and types of religious morphologies and "comparative" methods see Jonathan Z. Smith, "Adde Parvum Parvo Magnus Acervus Erit," _History of Religions_, XI, No. 1 (August, 1971), pp. 67-90.

27. Trans. Rosemary Sheed (Cleveland and New York: World Publishing Company, 1963). First published in French in 1949.

28. _CW_, 9, Part One, p. 183.

29. _Ibid._, p. 56.

30. _Ibid._

31. _Ibid._, p. 183.

32. _Ibid._

33. _Memories, Dreams, Reflections_, ed. by Aniela Jaffe, trans. Richard and Clara Winston (New York: Random House, 1961),   p. 200.

34. _Ibid._

35. _CW_, 18, p. 562.

36. _CW_, 9, Part One, p. 55.

37. _Ibid._, p. 56.

38. _Ibid._, pp. 56-57.

39. _CW_, 6, p. 527-528.

40. Cf. Eugene T. Gendlin, "Phenomenological Concept vs. Phenomenological Method: A Critique of Medard Boss on Dreams," _Soundings_, Vol. LX, No. 3 (Fall, 1977), pp. 285-300, for a discussion of these concepts in terms of Heidegger's point that phenomenology exists because phenomena are at first _not_ "given," and for a comparison of Boss and Jung on dream interpretation.

41. _CW_, 7, pp. 286ff.

42. _CW_, 6, p. 422.

43. _CW_, 7, pp. 79ff.

44. _Ibid._, p. 287.

45. _Ibid._.

46. _Collected Papers in Analytical Psychology_, ed. Constance E. Long (London: Baillière, Tindall and Cox, 1920), 2nd edition, p. 351.

47. _CW_, 18, p. 562.

48. For a study of the relationship of Jung and Eliade's work, including the influence of Jung on Eliade after 1950, see Mac Linscott Rickett's, "The Nature and Extent of Eliade's 'Jungianism'," _Union Seminary Quarterly Review_, Vol. XXV, No. 2 (Winter, 1970), pp. 211-234.

49. _Images and Symbols: Studies in Religious Symbolism_, trans. Philip Mairet (New York: Sheed and Ward, 1969), p. 35.

50. _CW_, 9, Part One, p. 168.

51. _Ibid._, p. 167.

52. _Ibid._, p. 170.

53. _Patterns in Comparative Religion_, p. 216.

54. _CW_, 9, Part One, p. 70.

55. C. G. Jung, _et. al._, _Man and His Symbols_ (New York: Dell Publishing Company, 1978), pp. 87-88.

56. Marie-Louise von Franz, _An Introduction to the Interpretation of Fairy Tales_ (New York: Spring Publications, 1970), p. 7.

57. _Ibid._.

58. For example, there is no evidence that Jung ever confronted Durkheim's critique of theories attempting to derive the "sacred-profane" dichotomy from individual rather than communal experience. Jung's only references to the French school are made in order to illustrate the idea of archetypes as a priori thought forms or

collective representations.

59. Peter Homans, *Jung in Context* (Chicago: University of Chicago Press, 1979), p. 199.

60. Extending the Jungian concept of an archetype into the social realm would be a direction rich with possibilities, particularly with regard to archetypes of the "sacred." Duty, honor, loyalty, and their many variant motifs are compelling, numinous structures which hold and foster great swaths of religious life. Within them, piety finds its most luxuriant flowerings and pathologies.

CHAPTER 4

JUNG AS GNOSTIC

Luther H. Martin

C. G. Jung fancied himself to be a descendant of
Goethe.1   Despite the questionableness of this
biological descent, the nature of his spiritual
descent is clear. As Goethe's Faust had made a pact
with Mephistopheles in order to realize a more
complete life, so Jung made a pact with his second or
inner self which allowed him to enter the
Walpurgisnacht of the unconscious. Jung was sustained
in this journey by his discovery of and relationship
with the feminine aspect of the Self, even as Faust
was sustained by his relationship with Helena. This
Faustian model of heroic exploration into the hidden
fullness of life, aided by the insight of the
feminine, is a Western paradigm of the self grounded
in the life of that traditional founder of Gnosticism,
Simon Magus, and his companion, Helen.2

Jung had read through the available Gnostic
writings as early as 1909, in the context of a general
interest in mythology, but he made little sense of
them.3   Then, in 1916, he published privately his
Septem Sermones ad Mortuos under the pseudonym of the
second century Gnostic writer, Basilides.4   This
poetic work gave expression, in Gnostic imagery, to
what became the central principle of Jung's
psychology, the compensatory union of opposites, light
and dark, male and female, within a pleromatic
fullness of origination and conclusion. Such an
undifferentiated union, psychologically formulated by
Jung in his view of the unconscious,5 was symbolized
for him by the "forgotten" Gnostic deity, Abraxas.
Jung understood this "Abraxian" or pleromatic nature

70

of man together with the differentiation of consciousness from it, as the structural basis of Gnostic expression, and this Gnostic structure became the basis for his understanding of the psyche.

From 1918 to 1926, Jung devoted himself to a more serious study of Gnosticism.6 By this time he had at his disposal the researches into Gnosticism of the German religionsgeschichtliche Schule.7 However, he turned his attention to the study of alchemy for, he concluded:

> alchemy formed the bridge on the one hand into the past, to Gnosticism, and on the other into the future, to the modern psychology of the unconscious.8

But, Jung never abandoned the Gnostic attitude of his Seven Sermons, and by 1951, in his mature work, Jung returned to a consideration of "Gnostic Symbols of the Self."9 When asked, shortly before his death, about his belief in God, he responded: "I don't need to believe, I know."10 This gnostic affirmation confirmed an attitude which permeated Jung's life and work from the beginning.

It is not surprising that Jung was fascinated especially by the Gnostic understanding of the Self. He cited Clement of Alexander, for example, who proclaimed that "it is the greatest of all disciplines to know oneself; for when a man knows himself, he knows God."11 Such Gnostic formulae supported Jung's view of the Self as an archetype of wholeness,12 and, consequently, as a God-image.13 In this way, Jung concluded that:

> Gnosis is undoubtedly a psychological knowledge whose contents derive from the unconscious.14

Or again:

> In Gnosticism we see man's unconscious psychology in full flower, almost perverse in its luxuriance.15

In the legends of Simon and Faust, the revelatory insights of their female companions redeemed them from

71

their luxuriant but chaotic condition. Jung understood these female companions psychologically as expressions of the feminine aspect of the Self, the anima, which communicates the fecund images of the unconscious to the conscious mind.16 Jung later conceded that his concept of the anima, looked at theologically, is pure Gnosticism.17

Jung found, then, in the mythological expressions of Gnosticism at the beginning of our era, the historical anticipation of and prefiguring for his psychological theory.18 Disillusioned with what he perceived as the narrow and blind faith of his father's Swiss Protestantism, he discovered in this Christian heresy the repressed side of orthodoxy, and thus an alternative expression of Western consciousness.19 As Gnosticism so eloquently stated, knowledge of the mythological was knowledge of the psychological, and through such knowledge, the psychikoi were completed, i.e., understood in their totality.20 The Gnostics, he wrote, had "recognized the necessity of some further raisonnement" absent in the Christian cosmos.21 This "gnostic" approach to religious expression may be identified as his concern to understand man's religious expression in its systemic totality, including its "dark" or repressed side,22 rather than in any desire to refute or to substantiate any religious position or belief.

In his later works, Jung was careful to distinguish between those second century C.E. historical traditions known as Gnosticism, and "Gnosis, as a special kind of knowledge."23 "I have Gnosis" he wrote, "so far as I have immediate experience, and my models are greatly helped by the représentations collectives of all religions (including Gnosticism)."24 With this distinction, he had sought to avoid any identification with particular ideological or theological positions.25 Jung wrote,

> I must confess that I myself could find access to religion only through the psychological understanding of inner experiences, whereas traditional religious interpretations left me high and dry.26

Similarly, from the perspective of the history of religions, Mircea Eliade has described the sacred as "an element in the structure of consciousness."27

As Jung understood not only Gnosticism but all religious expression in terms of its psychological dimension,28 the theological community in general reacted strongly. Martin Buber has offered perhaps the best known criticism of Jung's "heterodox" understanding.29 He charged Jung, first of all, with overstepping the boundaries of psychology by making metaphysical, i.e., theological statements, about the transcendent. Secondly, Buber accused Jung of proclaiming a "religion of Pure psychic immanance"30 by replacing the transcendent with the human soul. However, this charge seems to negate the first. And, Jung was historically correct in his observation of the decline of God imagery and the emergence of man imagery in modern consciousness.31

But the coup de grâce in Buber's attack was that Jung and his position were "Gnostic!"32 And, he argued:

> Gnosis is not to be understood as only a historical category, but as a universal one. It—and not atheism, which annihilates God because it must reject the hitherto existing images of God—is the real antagonist of the reality of faith.33

Jung had repeatedly insisted that he spoke only about the indisputably psychological aspect of religious expression,34 and the substance of his "Reply to Martin Buber" is a reiteration of this position.35 As a psychologist, he was not concerned with "the reality of faith" in Buber's sense; rather he was interested in the psychological meaning of doctrinal reality. Consequently, while Jung's understanding of religion was unorthodox, it did not deprecate such faith. Thus, he could conclude his work on "Psychology and Religion" with the admonition that "only heedless fools will wish to destroy this [Christian dogma]; the lover of the soul never."36

Out of this same desire to understand the underlying psychological meaning of doctrinal or confessional reality, it is equally true that Jung's psychological position could not become a substitute religion as Buber had charged and as many Jungians themselves have advocated.37 Rather, Jung's "gnostic" approach led to an exploration of those archetypal structures underlying psychological "dogma" as well.38

Jung's psychological interpretation of Gnosticism, then, offered along with the better known existential-phenomenological interpretation of his contemporary, Rudolf Bultmann, and Bultmann's student, Hans Jonas,39 an alternative model for understanding religious expressions to those shaped by theological presupposition or psychological reduction. Wayne Meeks has suggested that the Jungian concept of myth as projection giving expression to unconscious processes, i.e., to Self in its totality, "is significantly parallel" to the Jonas-Bultmann understanding of myth as the objectification of man's understanding of his existence.40 This relationship has been suggestively worked out by James Goss.41

Meeks and Goss, however, have overlooked a crucial difference between Jung's and Bultmann's theories of myth. Whereas Jung understood myth as expressions of trans-historical and trans-cultural patterns of the psyche, Bultmann understood myth in terms of its particular historical setting as expressions of man's existential situation.42 Consequently, Jung interpreted mythological expression archetypally, in terms of its universal structures, whereas Bultmann understood the historical particularity of mythological expression as decisive. Jung's therapeutic aim to withdraw individual projections from the universality of mythic expression is the opposite of Bultmann's demythologizing of a particular mythic objectification to its common existential meaning. To cite Guilford Dudley's cogent formulation, Bultmann wants to demythologize text into history and then into existential encounter. "Eliade [and here we can read Jung] wants to remythologize history into mythic text and then into existential encounter as defined by the myth."43 Thus, Bultmann argues a radically historical theory of myth in contrast to Jung's universal, and thus normalizing project.

For the student of religion, then, Jung's work offers an interpretation of religion to a psychological--some would say Gnostic--age44 which he intended as neither reductionistic in the traditional sense nor theological in its orientation. It does assume both the validity and the universality of his psychological model--finally, an acceptance of the archetype of individuation. However, it is a model which Jung sought to ground in, rather than impose upon, such historical examples as Gnosticism and alchemy. His understandings, especially of alchemy, have been favorably received both by historians of religion and by historians of science.45 The student of religion who is concerned neither with theological nor with psychological truth, but in the expressions of man's religious life as data for his investigations, may well learn from the heuristic and pedagogical possibilities suggested by the gnostic attitude of Jung and his circle.

1. C. G. Jung, _Memories, Dreams, Reflections,_ recorded and edited by Aniela Jaffe, translated by Richard and Clara Winston (New York: Vintage Books, 1963), p. 35 and n.

2. See Gilles Quispel, "Faust: Symbol of Western Man," in _Gnostic Studies,_ 2 vols. (Leiden: Nederlands Historisch-Archaelogisch Instituut te Istanbul, 1975,) vol. 2, pp. 288-307.

3. _Memories, Dreams, Reflections, op. cit.,_ p. 162.

4. Trans. and published as "Appendix V," _Memories, Dreams, Reflections, ibid.,_ pp. 378-390. See also Stephan A. Hoeller, _The Gnostic Jung_ (Wheaton, Illinois, Madras, London: The Theosophical Publishing House, 1982), pp. 44-58 and 219f.

5. E.g., C. G. Jung, _Aion,_ trans. R.F.C. Hull, CW 9, ii, 2nd edition (Princeton: Princeton University Press, 1968), p. 193.

6. _Memories, Dreams, Reflections, op. cit.,_ pp. 200f.

7. E.g., Albrecht Dieterich's pioneering work, _Eine Mithrasliturgie,_ published in 1903, followed by Richard Reitzenstein's _Poimandres_ in 1904, Wilhelm Bousset's _Hauptprobleme der Gnosis_ in 1907, and in 1910, Wolfgang Schultz's _Dokumente der Gnosis_ and Reitzenstein's _Die hellenistischen Mysterienreligionen._

8. _Memories, Dreams, Reflections, op. cit.,_ pp. 200-201.

9. _Aion, op. cit.,_ pp. 184-221.

10. BBC interview with John Freeman, 1959; cited by Wallace B. Clift, _Jung and Christianity_ (New York: Crossroad, 1982), p. 3.

11. _Paedagogus_ III, 1, cited by Jung, _Aion, ibid.,_ p. 222.

12. _Ibid._, p. 223.

13. _Ibid._, p. 22.

14. _Ibid._, p. 223.

15. C. G. Jung, _Psychological Types_, trans. H. G. Baynes, rev. R. F. C. Hull, CW 6 (Princeton: Princeton University Press, 1971), pp. 241f.

16. _Memories, Dreams, Reflections, op. cit._, pp. 187-189.

17. _Psychology and Religon: West and East_, trans. R. F. C. Hull, CW 11, 2nd ed. (Princeton: Princeton University Press, 1969), p. 306.

18. _Aion, op. cit._, p. 184.

19. Gilles Quispel, _Gnosis als Weltreligion_ (Zurich: Origio Verlag, 1972), pp. 76-77.

20. _Psychology and Religion: West and East, op. cit._, p. 96n.

21. _The Symbolic Life_, trans. R. F. C. Hull, CW 18 (Princeton: Princeton University Press, 1976), p. 728.

22. "The Gnostics have the merit of having raised the problem of _pothen to kakon;_ [whence evil?]." _The Symbolic Life, ibid.,_ p. 727.

23. _Psychology and Religion: East and West, op. cit.,_ p. 45n; this same distinction was made by the participants in the colloquim on _The Origins of Gnosticism_, ed. Ugo Bianchi (Leiden: E. J. Brill, 1967), p. xxvii.

24. _The Symbolic Life, op. cit.,_ p. 728.

25. _Psychology and Religion: West and East, op. cit.,_ pp. 306f.

26. _The Symbolic Life, op. cit.,_ p. 728.

27. _The Quest,_ (Chicago and London: The University of Chicago Press, 1969), "Preface."

28. _Psychology_ and _Religion:_ _West_ and _East,_ _op._ _cit.,_ p. 80.

29. Martin Buber, _Eclipse_ _of_ _God_ (New York: Harper & Row, 1957), pp. 78-119, 133-137.

30. Buber, _op._ _cit.,_ p. 84.

31. M.-L. von Franz, _C._ _G._ _Jung,_ _His_ _Myth_ _in_ _our_ _Time_ (London, Sydney, Auckland, Toronto: Hodder and Stoughton, 1975), pp. 188-189.

32. Buber, _op._ _cit.,_ pp. 84-85.

33. _Ibid.,_ p. 136.

34. E.g., _Psychology_ _and_ _Alchemy,_ _op._ _cit.,_ pp. 13-14; and _Psychology_ _and_ _Religion:_ _West_ _and_ _East,_ _op._ _cit.,_ p. 85.

35. "Religion and Psychology: A Reply to Martin Buber," _The_ _Symbolic_ _Life,_ _op._ _cit.,_ pp. 663-670.

36. _Psychology_ _and_ _Religion:_ _West_ _and_ _East,_ _op._ _cit.,_ p. 107.

37. E.g., Edward F. Edinger, _Ego_ _and_ _Archetype_ (New York: G. P. Putnam's Sons, 1972), p. 105.

38. The exploration of those archetypes underlying Jung's psychology itself is the work assumed primarily by James Hillman, esp. _Re-Visioning_ _Psychology_ (New York, Evanston, San Francisco, London: Harper & Row, 1975).

39. _Gnosis_ _und_ _Spaetantiker_ _Geist,_ _Erster_ _Teil:_ _Die_ _mythologische_ _Gnosis_ (Goettingen: Vandenhoeck & Ruprecht, 1964), esp. pp. 84-90; and _The_ _Gnostic_ _Religion,_ 2nd ed. rev. (Boston: Beacon Press, 1963).

40. "The Man from Heaven in Johannine Sectarianism," _Journal_ _of_ _Biblical_ _Literature_ 91 (1972), p. 47, n. 10.

41. _Infra,_ Chapter 6.

42. For example, see in the new translation of some key essays by Rudolf Bultmann, _New_ _Testament_ _and_ _Mythology_ _and_ _Other_ _Basic_ _Writings,_ trans.

Schubert M. Ogden (Philadelphia: Fortress Press, 1984), pp. 3, 35, and especially on p. 95: "I understand by 'myth' a very specific historical phenomenon and by 'mythology' a very specific mode of thinking."

43. Guilford Dudley, _Religion on Trial: Mircea Eliade & His Critics_ (Philadelphia: Temple University Press, 1977), p.

44. Jonas, "Epilogue," to _The Gnostic Religion_, _op. cit._, pp. 320-340.

45. E.g., Gilles Quispel; see Eliade, _op. cit._, p. 226.

SECTION II

APPLICATIONS OF JUNGIAN PSYCHOLOGY
TO THE STUDY OF RELIGION

CHAPTER 5

JUNG ON SCRIPTURE AND HERMENEUTICS:

RETROSPECT AND PROSPECT

Wayne G. Rollins

In his preface to _Answer to Job_, Jung provides a key for understanding the role of Scripture in his life and thought. Jung states: "I do not write as a biblical scholar (which I am not), but as a layman and a physician who has been privileged to see deeply into the psychic life of many people."1 This statement corroborates Peter Homan's thesis in _Jung in Context: Modernity and the Making of a Psychology_,2 that the analysis and appraisal of Jung's thought is best done by noting its place in the context of Jung's personal life, which should include not only his relationship with his family, his reaction to traditional Christianity, his break with Freud, and his view of the role of religion in our culture as a "counterbalance to mass-mindedness"--as Homans suggests, but also for our purposes, his personal agenda. Jung refers to this agenda in _Memories, Dreams, Reflections_ as his "main business" and describes it thus: "My life has been permeated and held together by one idea and one goal: namely, to penetrate into the secret of the personality. Everything can be explained from this central point, and all my works relate to this one theme."3

Accepting these contextual factors as critical for interpreting Jung's _curriculum vitae_, our purpose here is to provide an overview of the role Scripture plays in this _curriculum_. Jung shows keen interest in the contribution Scripture makes to the life of the psyche, specifically among persons rooted in the West, both in its adverse as well as constructive effects.

We will comment on three aspects of the role of Scripture in Jung's life and thought: (a) Jung's actual use of Scripture, professionally and personally, and its ubiquity in his life and thought; (b) Jung's attitude toward the method and result of critical Biblical scholarship; and (c) Jung's understanding of Scripture as sacred text. We will conclude with observations on some programmatic implications of the foregoing for a future hermeneutic.

Jung's Use of Scripture, Professionally and Personally

At first glance, the Jungian corpus provides little evidence of Jung's interest in Scripture. _Answer_ _to_ _Job_, written in 1952, is the most conspicuous testimony to Jung's Biblical interests and is the only work of Jung's devoted solely to the discussion of a Biblical text.

However, as one ruminates through the _Collected_ _Works_ one uncovers a thesaurus of Biblical passages, personages, phrases, images, and concepts. In the course of the twenty volumes Jung manages to refer to all but thirteen of the sixty-six books of the Biblical canon. In addition he cites inter-testamental writings, e.g. Slavonic Enoch, II Esdras, and Tobit, along with works from the Apocryphal New Testament, e.g. the Gospel of Philip, the Acts of Peter and the Book of the Apostle Bartholomew. He even betrays a seasoned familiarity with the nuanced observations of the textual critic, remarking on the variant textual versions of the dominical sayings.

In addition one finds a glossary of Biblical names, expressions, and terms. Adam and Abraham, Peter and Job, Elijah and Salome appear along with dozens from the cast of characters that populate the Biblical narrative and symbolize Biblical experience. The weighted Biblical images of the "inner man," the pharisee and the publican, and of the "spirit searching the deep things of God" (I Cor. 2:10) surface with remarkable naturalness in Jung's essays and letters. Repeatedly Jung makes clear his recognition of the power of these figures to touch the

depths of the soul and to give voice to the depths of
human experience with impressive and probing accuracy.
Jung confesses familiarity with the wounding and
binding up that Job experienced at the hand of God; he
identifies with Abraham and Paul who went against the
storm; and on his tomb-stone he chose to have
inscribed not only the words of the Pythian oracle,
"Vocatus atque non vocatus Deus aderit" ("Summoned or
not summoned, God will be present"), but also words of
the apostle Paul: "Primus homo terrenus de terra;
secundus homo coelestis de coelo" ("the first man is
of the earth, a man of dust; the second is of heaven")
(I Cor. 15:47).

Beyond these explicit allusions to Biblical
expression, one should mention Jung's general approach
to experience that reflects what might be labelled a
Biblical _Weltanschauung_ (though certainly not a
Biblical _Weltbild_). Jung exhibits in his work an
angle of vision that renders visible many of the
Biblical realities that have been rendered virtually
invisible from a rationalistic perspective. The
realities and experience that count most in Jung's
internal biography are those that occupy primary
attention in the writings of the Biblical authors,
e.g., an awareness of the numinous depth of life; a
sense of _vocatio_; a responsiveness to the wisdom of
dreams and visions; and a seasoned sense of the
paradox that "where sin is great, grace abounds."

Scripture is a central reality for Jung,
imaginally and thematically; and though it never
emerges as a subject for concentrated critical comment
from a psychological perspective aside from **Answer to
Job**, it appears to be a fundamental factor in Jung's
personal and professional vocabulary as he pursues his
"main business."

Jung's Attitude Toward the Method and Result
of Critical Biblical Scholarship

In his Terry Lectures at Yale in 1937, Jung makes
a passing observation that is probably his most
explicit commentary on critical Biblical scholarship.
He writes:

Nor has the scientific criticism of the New
Testament been very helpful in enhancing the
divine character of the holy writings. It
is also a fact that under the influence of

so-called scientific enlightenment great
masses of educated people have either left
the church or have become profoundly
indifferent to it.

And he adds, "if they were all dull rationalists or
neurotic intellectuals the loss would not be
regrettable. But many of them are religious people,
only incapable of agreeing with the actually existing
forms of creed."4

One might gather from this that Jung is
unsympathetic with the historical-literary-critical
analysis of sacred texts. This is hardly the case.
Reading in the Jungian corpus one is continually
impressed not only with Jung's mastery of Greek and
Latin texts ranging from the New Testament and
Apostolic Fathers to the medieval church, but with his
familiarity with literary-critical issues and with his
native talent for what would be regarded by
contemporary scholars as a serious and informed
historical-critical approach.

An instance of this approach surfaces in a letter
Jung wrote the American writer, Upton Sinclair, who
had solicited Jung's opinion on his new novel, A
Personal Jesus. Jung begins with reference to the
earlier attempts of Strauss, Renan and Schweitzer to
write about the historical Jesus, as preamble to his
comments on Sinclair's work. Acknowledging that A
Personal Jesus might "be convincing to a modern
American mind," Jung contends that

. . . seen from the standpoint of a European
scientist, your modus procedendi seems to be
a bit too selective; . . . you exclude too
many authentic statements for no other
reason than that they do not fit in with
your premises.

"They cannot be dismissed as mere interpolations," he
writes.

We can learn from your book what a modern
American writer 'thinks about Jesus'. . . .
We can draw a portrait of Jesus that does
not offend our rationalism, but it is done
at the expense of our loyalty to the textual
authority. As a matter of fact, we can omit
nothing from the authentic text. We cannot

84

create a true picture of Hermetic philosophy in the IVth century if we dismiss half of the *libelli* contained in the *Corpus Hermeticum*. The New Testament as it stands is the 'Corpus Christianum,' which is to be accepted as a whole or not at all. We can dismiss nothing that stands up to a reasonable philological critique.5

The point, however, that Jung makes to Sinclair in the end is that no satisfactory "rational" portrait of Jesus can ever be constructed from the text, not because of the complex historical problems, but because "the Gospels do not give, and do not even intend to give a biography of the Lord."6 The Gospel is less a biographical portrait of the historical Jesus than it is testimony to the Christological impact of Jesus within the lives of the Gospel writers and their communities. Jung contends "we cannot unravel a rational story" from the Gospels unless we interfere with the texts, because the story the Gospel tells is of "the life, fate, and effect of a God-man."7 To gain insight into such a text it is necessary to go beyond the methods and assumptions of rational-historicism to develop a conceptual perspective and method equal to the task of grappling with the fundamentally arational effect of the historical Jesus upon the earliest Christians and with the congeries of stories, symbols, and images generated in that experience and eventually gathered as "gospel."

Thus although Jung endorses scientific criticism of Scripture for its method and rigor, he faults it for the narrowness of its line of inquiry. Commenting in analogous fashion on popular response to the promulgation of the dogma of the Assumption in 1950 (another "religious text"), Jung observes that the newspaper and professional journal articles assessing this event were "satisfied with learned considerations, dogmatic and historical, which," Jung contends, "have no bearing on the living religious process."8 "Arguments based on historical criticism will never do justice to the new dogma," Jung maintains, because they are "out of touch with the tremendous archetypal happenings in the psyche of the individual and the masses" which provide what Jung calls the psychological "need" or occasion for such a dogma. *Mutatis mutandis,* an *exclusively* historical-critical approach to Scripture is also out of touch with the "tremendous archetypal happenings" Scripture has generated and continues to generate in the psyche of individuals and communities.9

Jung anticipates a breed of Biblical critics who would not be content with studying Scripture (or dogma) simply as part of an historical or literary process. They would be willing to reflect on it also as part of a psychic or psychological process, that is, as a constellation of laws and apocalypses, epistles and gospels, psalms and prophecy, etc., that appeared in written form because of their archetypal significance for the scriptural authors and their communities, and that continued to be preserved and read because of their archetypal significance for the readers and their communities. In both instances they follow rules of the psyche that are inaccessible to mere historical-critical assessment.10

Jung's Understanding of Scripture as Sacred Text

At a time when Biblical criticism was drawing attention to the Bible's rootedness in history, Jung was reflecting on the rootedness of Scripture in the human psyche or soul. Commenting on a passage in Tertullian's _De testimonio animae_, in which he speaks of the soul as the "mistress" of God and "diviner for men," Jung states, "I would go a step further and say that the statements made in the Holy Scriptures are also utterances of the soul." What Jung intends is elaborated as follows:

> . . . religious statements are psychic confessions which in the last resort are based on unconscious, i.e., on transcendental processes. These processes are not accessible to physical perception but demonstrate their existence through the confessions of the psyche. . . . Whenever we speak of religious contents we move in a world of images that point to something ineffable. We do not know how clear or unclear these images, metaphors, and concepts are in respect of their transcendental object. . . . I am also too well aware of how limited are our powers of conception. . . . But, although our whole world of religious ideas consists of anthropomorphic images that could never stand up to rational criticism, we should

never forget that they are based on numinous
archetypes, i.e., on . . . [a] foundation
which is unassailable by reason. We are
dealing with psychic facts which logic can
overlook but not eliminate.11

Thus, although as a professional psychologist
Jung does not regard himself competent to speak of the
sacrality of Scripture as a metaphysical fact, he does
speak of its quintessentially spiritual or soulful
character as a psychological fact. In so doing, Jung
reminds the critical scholarly community that the text
is not to be examined primarily as a source of
information on social, historical, cultic, or
linguistic matters, but as a source of insight into
the nature of the soul, its images, its visions, and
its truths. The primary subject matter of Scripture
is numinous; its primary raison d'etre resides in the
realm of the psycho-spiritual; and its main business
is "soul-making."12 It is with these objective
qualities of Scripture in mind that Jung can speak to
his scientific colleagues in psychology and Biblical
criticism of the "divine character of the holy
writings," drawing their attention not only to the
special psycho-spiritual genre Scripture represents
but also the special hermeneutical approach this
reality recommends. The purpose of Scripture in
Jung's judgment is not primarily to inform the mind,
but, to borrow a phrase from D. H. Lawrence, "to
change the blood." Jung would hold that a
Biblical-critical strategy failing to recognize this
fact is apt to miss the point.

Implications for a Future Hermeneutic

Jung once commented, "to gain an understanding of
religious matters, probably all that is left us today
is the psychological approach."13 Though the
statement may appear shamelessly bold, it does reflect
an insight gaining acceptance even within
Biblical-critical circles. In a 1968 Festschrift
article honoring Erwin R. Goodenough, F. C. Grant,
classicist and New Testament scholar writes:

Dr. Goodenough pointed out the value and
importance, even the necessity, of the
psychological interpretation of the Bible.
This is a new kind of biblical criticism.
The earlier disciplines, Textual Criticism,
Historical Criticism, Source Criticism, and

Form Criticism, are all parts of or stages in Literary Criticism, necessary and important and not to be ignored. But Psychological Criticism opens up a wholly new and vast, far-reaching scene where the creative function of tradition and writing is fully recognized but where the real incentive comes from a far deeper spring, viz. the immediate testimony of the religious consciousness. . . . In a word, beyond the historical and exegetical interpretation of the Bible lies the whole new field of depth psychology and psychoanalysis.14

Fifteen years earlier Henry Cadbury made a comparable observation, expressing the hunch that New Testament research may in time proceed from questions of origin, date, and authorship to questions of "culture and Weltanschauung." "To put it bluntly," Cadbury writes, "I find myself much more intrigued with curiosity about how the New Testament writers got that way than with knowing who they were." Suggesting that the key issues in Biblical interpretation are often "psychological rather than literary," he writes, "it is regrettable that so little has been done and is being done to match the study of expression with a study of mind and experience."15 And more recently, in 1975, Peter Stuhlmacher in Historical Criticism and Theological Interpretation of Scripture proposes that historical critics take the necessary steps to find a way of measuring

to what degree we actually need additional psychological and sociological, even linguistic categories and methods of interpretation to broaden and give precision to our understanding of tradition.16

Traditionally, of course, Biblical scholarship has regarded any attempt to apply psychological insight to Biblical analysis with suspicion. What is often overlooked, however, is that the risk of applying psychological insight to scriptural interpretation is in principle no greater than that of applying historical or literary-critical insight. In all cases the risk is the same, namely of submitting to the temptation of reducing the Biblical text to nothing but a psychological, or historical, or literary phenomenon. Jung himself warns against this possibility. In his essay "On the Relation of Analytical Psychology to Poetry" he writes that:

in the realm of religion . . . a psychological approach is permissible only in regard to the emotions and symbols which constitute the phenomenology of religion, but which do not touch upon its essential nature. If the essence of religion and art could be explained, then both of them would become mere subdivisions of psychology. This is not to say that such violations of their nature have not been attempted. But those who are guilty of them obviously forget that a similar fate might easily befall psychology, since its intrinsic value and specific quality would be destroyed if it were regarded as a mere activity of the brain.

Applying this observation to the psychological analysis of art, Jung counsels,

. . . Art by its very nature is not science, and science by its very nature is not art. . . . If a work of art is explained in the same way as a neurosis, then either the work of art is a neurosis or a neurosis is a work of art. . . .

In summary, Jung maintains,

Psychology has only a modest contribution to make toward a deeper understanding of the phenomena of life and is no nearer than its sister sciences to absolute knowledge.17

But, he would insist, it nevertheless has a contribution to make.

What are some of the programmatic suggestions Jung's insight into Scripture might make for the ongoing work of Biblical scholarship and hermeneutics?

First, the Biblical scholar might consider the exegetical implications of regarding the text not only as a product of an historical, theological, literary, and linguistic process, but also as the product of a psychic process, pondering what the human psyche in its conscious and unconscious dimensions is and how it functions, not only as a factor in the life of the Biblical author and his community, but also in the life and work of the Biblical reader and his community and in the continuing history of the reception and interpretation of the text. As Jung observes,

> No matter how low anyone's opinion of the unconscious may be, he must concede that it is worth investigation; the unconscious is at least on the level with the louse, which, after all, enjoys the honest interest of the entomologist.18

If there is reason to believe that unconscious factors play a role in the emergence of Scripture along with the habits of human consciousness into which psychology and psychoanalysis have given us insight, it behooves Biblical scholarship to spend some time coming to terms with these realities.

Second, the Biblical scholar might consider the exegetical implications of regarding the text as a bearer of symbols, laden not only with the meanings they have accrued in the writer's personal unconscious, but also with the meanings they negotiate in a broader, species-wide, or collective sense. As Jung points out, "even the most commonplace of images or objects can assume powerful psychic significance." For the Biblical critic to ignore this fact is to risk insensitivity to the range of meanings a text inevitably conveys, some of which are consciously intended by the author and consciously registered by the reader, but others of which are conveyed apart from the conscious intention of author and reader alike, and in some instances may not surface for generations until a readership appears ready to receive them.19

Third, in an attempt to understand Biblical symbols and images in their psychological depth, Biblical scholars might consider undertaking the task of amplifying their already rich collection of comparative archaeological, historical, and linguistic data, by adding comparative mythological and symbolic data, in an attempt to enhance our understanding of the range of potential values a given Biblical symbol might convey.

Fourth, Biblical scholarship might examine Jung's psychology of archetypes with respect to coming to a clearer understanding of the phenomenon of the catalytic effect the Biblical story can have on its readers. The angle of vision that archetypal psychology provides, with its proposal that humans in all times and places tend to voice their experience of fundamental life situations with a cast of stock-images that recur in the stories, fairy tales, myths, dreams, and legends around the world, suggests that new light might be cast for the Biblical scholar on the riddle of the astonishingly rapid spread of the Christian kerygma in the first century of the Christian era. Biblical scholars in the past have sought to account for the phenomenon in everything but psychological terms. They have traced it to historical, economic, intellectual, and social causes, all the while ignoring the fact that the phenomenon of the kerygma and the kerygmatic event is above all, to use Jung's terminology, a psychic event or an event in the life of the soul, and should be examined from this perspective.20

Fifth, Biblical hermeneutics might also consider Jung's proposal that one of the primary ways to interpret a text is to "dream the myth on." Applied to scriptural scholarship this would entail a renewed study of and a more empathetic approach to the Rabbinic and medieval methods of allegory, anagogy, and tropology as modes of unpacking and amplifying the meaning of a text in a way consonant with the original intent of the Biblical authors, a fact that contemporary form-critical scholarship is helping us to see in its insight into the fact that the text was originally intended not simply as a document of record, but as a sacred text to be used and amplified in the worshipping, teaching, and preaching life of the community.21

To return to the beginning, Jung does not pretend to write as a Biblical scholar, "but as a layman and a physician who has been privileged to see deeply into the psychic life of many people." But the Biblical scholar can benefit from his insight and as a result probe with greater consciousness into the soulful life of the text, the author, the community of interpreters past and present, and his or her own self.

1. C. G. Jung, The Collected Works of C. G. Jung, Vol. XI, ed. Gerhard Adler, Michael Fordham, Sir Herbert Read, and William McGuire; trans. R. F. C. Hull, Bollingen Series XX (Princeton: Princeton University Press, 1953-78), p. 363.

2. (Chicago: University of Chicago Press, 1979)

3. Ed. Aniela Jaffe; trans. Richard and Clara Winston (New York: Pantheon, 1963), p. 206.

4. "Psychology and Religion" in Collected Works, XI, pp. 21-22.

5. C. G. Jung, C. G. Jung Letters, I-II, ed. Gerhard Adler and Aniela Jaffe, Bollingen Series XCV (Princeton: Princeton University Press, 1973-75), II, p. 88.

6. Ibid., p. 90.

7. Ibid., p. 89.

8. "Answer to Job," Collected Works, XI, p. 461.

9. For an overview of the occurrences and functions of the term psyche in the New Testament corpus, cf. Wayne G. Rollins, Jung and the Bible (Atlanta: John Knox Press, 1983), pp. 45f.

10. It should be noted that structural criticism has addressed some of the issues Jung identifies. Approaching the text not only as an informational entity, but as a meaning-bearing entity, structural criticism explores the "system of deep values or convictions" implicit in a text that exercise a "meaning effect" on the reader. But as Daniel and Aline Patte observe in Structural Exegesis: From Theory to Practice (Philadelphia: Fortress Press, 1978), p. 12, structural exegesis "makes no pretense of being an objective description of the manner in which aspects of meaning are produced and apprehended by the human mind." To explore such phenomena will require

critical methods and approaches other than those of the structural critic; cf. _infra_, "Implications for a Future Hermeneutic."

11. "Answer to Job," _Collected Works_, XI, pp. 360-62.

12. Cf. Rollins, _Jung and the Bible_, pp. 97f., commenting on 2 Tim. 3:16-17.

13. "Psychology and Religion," _Collected Works_, XI, par. 148, cited in Edward F. Edinger, _Ego and Archetype_ (Baltimore: Penguin Books, Inc., 1973), p. 131.

14. "Psychological Study of the Bible," in Jacob Neusner, ed., _Religions in Antiquity_: _Essays in Memory of Erwin Ramsdell Goodenough_, _Numen_, Spl. XIV (Leiden: Brill, 1969), pp. 112f.

15. "Current Issues in New Testament Study," Harvard Divinity School Bulletin, p. 54, cited in Howard C. Kee, _Christian Origins in Sociological Perspective_ (Philadelphia: Westminster Press, 1980), p. 11.

16. (Philadelphia: Fortress Press, 1977), p. 86. Cf. also G. B. Caird, _The Language and Imagery of the Bible_ (Philadelphia: Westminster Press, 1980), p. vii, who cites the need for psychological as well as linguistic, anthropological, philosophical and theological expertise in approaching the study of Biblical language.

17. "On the Relation of Analytical Psychology to Poetry," in _The Portable Jung_, ed. Joseph Campbell (New York: Viking Press, 1971), pp. 302ff.

18. C. G. Jung, "Approaching the Unconscious," in C. G. Jung, _et. al._, _Man and His Symbols_ (New York: Doubleday and Company, 1971), p. 32.

19. With respect to the latter point, cf. Hans Robert Jauss, "Literary History as a Challenge to Literary Theory," in Ralph Cohen, ed., _New Directions in Literary History_ (Baltimore: Johns Hopkins Press, 1974), p. 31, who speaks of a "new phase of literary evaluation" that may "unexpectedly" illumine past works.

20. Cf., for example, Jung's statement that "Christ would never have made the impression he did on his followers if he had not expressed something that was alive and at work in their unconscious. Christianity itself would never have spread through the pagan world with such astonishing rapidity had its ideas not found an analogous psychic readiness to receive them," in "Answer to Job," <u>Collected Works</u>, XI, p. 441.

21. Cf. the observation of James Wiggins in <u>Religion as Story</u> (New York: Harper and Row, 1976), p. 9: "Origen, Clement, Jerome, and Augustine, reflected their training in the rhetorical, satirical, and allegorical traditional forms of the Greeks, as well as an immersion in the stories preserved in the sacred writing. We have tended in historical studies to focus on the rationalistic theologizing through which the intelligentsia were wooed to Christianity. Correspondingly, we have been less sensitive to the quantitatively far greater tradition through which the masses encountered Christian communication--sermons, commentaries, romances, legends, lives of the saints, and histories. . . ."

CHAPTER 6

ESCHATOLOGY, AUTONOMY, AND INDIVIDUATION: THE

EVOCATIVE POWER OF THE KINGDOM

James Goss

The eschatological significance of Jesus' proclamation of the Kingdom of God has been the subject of debate by New Testament scholars since the publication in 1892 of Johannes Weiss's _Die Predigt Jesu vom Reiche Gottes_. The work of those in the history of religions school confirmed Weiss's work by establishing the supernatural element in Jesus' preaching. According to that view the coming of the Kingdom is exclusively the work of God, who from "beyond" the world suddenly breaks into the course of history to end it. Consequently, the Kingdom is not a continuous process of natural growth and maturation leading to the perfection of human moral or spiritual character, but the radical denial of such possibilities. The Kingdom is not concerned with inwardness in the soul, but with a transformation of the cosmos in which human existence is judged and God's reign of grace established.

Rudolf Bultmann, one of Weiss's pupils and the leading voice in twentieth-century New Testament scholarship, states:

> The Kingdom of God is not an ideal which realizes itself in human history; we cannot speak of its founding, its building, its completion; we can say only that it draws near, it comes, it appears. It is

95

supernatural, superhistorical; and while men
can "receive" its salvation, can enter it,
it is not _they_, with their fellowship and
their activity, who constitute the Kingdom,
but God's salvation alone.1

According to Bultmann, subjectivistic
misunderstandings of the Kingdom are based upon the
so-called "parables of growth," such as the parable of
the sower, where it appears that organic development
is analogous to the growth of the Kingdom. But these
parables, Bultmann and most New Testament scholars
argue, are not concerned with human development;
rather, they depict the inescapability and suddenness
of the coming Kingdom as God's own work. Armed with
the results of his teachers, Bultmann attacks
nineteenth-century assumptions of the moral or
spiritual character of the Kingdom and insists that
for Jesus the Kingdom rejects "all humanistic
individualism," since it has nothing to do with the
realization of latent capacities in the self. He
claims: "All individualistic cultivation of the
spirit, all mysticism, is exluded. Jesus calls to
decision, not to the inner life."2 Because of the
eschatological character of the Kingdom, entos humon
in Luke 17:21 is translated "among you," not "within
you," to avoid any subjectivistic misunderstanding.

C. G. Jung, who spent his life illuminating the
inner process of individual development, argues that
individuation, the thrust toward wholeness, is
essential for those who pursue "a high ideal, an idea
of the best we can do."3 This pursuit, Jung claims,
is "at the same time the primitive Christian ideal of
the Kingdom of Heaven which 'is within you'."4 The
denial that the Kingdom is an inner aspect of the self
Jung attributes to the extraverted stance of Western
scholars, whose focus on the outward aspect of the
ideal--Christ--blinds them to the Kingdom's
"mysterious relation to the inner man."5 "It is this
prejudice," Jung continues, "which impels the
Protestant interpreters of the Bible to interpret
entos humon (referring to the Kingdom of God) as
'among you' instead of 'within you'." Jung, who
demonstrates little awareness of critical discussions
among New Testament scholars, defends his assumption
that both Christ and his Kingdom are "within" by
referring to the parable of the sower, which he says
makes explicit "the likeness of the Kingdom of God to
man."6

The antithetical views of Bultmann and Jung on the nature of the Kingdom appear to block a rapprochement between New Testament scholars, such as Bultmann, and Jungian psychology. Yet if we develop more fully how Bultmann and his followers interpret Jesus' eschatological language, we will discover that Jung's understanding of the nature and function of symbol enriches the discussion among New Testament scholars and discloses facets of the Kingdom of God that might otherwise remain hidden.

Unlike Weiss, who discovered the eschatological nature of Jesus' preaching of the Kingdom only to reject its relevance for theology, Bultmann believes that behind Jesus' mythological statements lies a valid understanding of human existence. For Bultmann,

> the real purpose of myth is not to present an objective picture of the world as it is, but to express man's understanding of himself in the world in which he lives. Myth should be interpreted not cosmologically, but anthropologically, or better still, existentially.7

The program of demythologizing presupposes that myth is the objectification in language of a person's understanding of existence.

Jesus, according to Bultmann, shared with his contemporaries a belief in a catastrophic event that would end history, an event in which the "Son of Man" would descend from heaven riding on clouds to sit in judgment upon those risen from the dead. Some of those judged would be granted the glory of heaven, while for others there would be the torments of hell. While, in contrast to other apocalypticists, Jesus did not utilize elaborate portraits of other-worldly events, nor permit any speculation about the signs of time of the Kingdom's coming, nevertheless, Bultmann is convinced that Jesus' mythological language is incompatible with quantum mechanics of Einstein's universe. What, then, is the existential import of Jesus' eschatology according to Bultmann?

For Bultmann the significance of the eschatological message of Jesus is that it places a person in a crisis of decision which discloses the true nature of the self. "If men are standing in the crisis of decision," he states, "and if precisely this crisis is the essential characteristic of their humanity, then every hour is the last hour, and we can understand that for Jesus the whole contemporary mythology is pressed into the service of this conception of human existence."8 Jesus' preaching reveals that a person is not a fixed or permanent entity, but is ever the result of new decisions. One's self, therefore, is not found by inward reflection, but by responding continuously to new encounters.

The eschatological nature of the Kingdom guards against identifying the activity of God with any human work or quality. As Bultmann states, "the fulfillment of human life cannot be the result of human effort but is rather a gift from beyond, the gift of God's grace."9 The Kingdom is autonomous. It is not subject to human control; it is an invitation and a demand, and it ripens "without human agency or understanding."10 Bultmann's denial that the Kingdom has to do with inwardness, or mysticism, or human growth rests upon the eschatological factor in Jesus' language.

Since mythological language hides its meaning from modern understanding--that is to say, since it is an objectification of an understanding of human existence--Bultmann seeks to get behind eschatological utterances, which when demythologized are understandable. This view of language has been challenged by Bultmann's pupils. Utilizing Heidegger's later writings on language, those in the "new Hermeneutic" argue that language does not hide, but creates the possibility of encounter or participation. The program of the "new hermeneutic," therefore, is to focus on the understanding of language, not on an understanding of existence postulated to lie behind it. This shift of emphasis means that in regard to the eschatology of the Kingdom, one does not seek Jesus' existential experience prior to his formulation of it in language, but rather one demonstrates how his language brings the Kingdom into being.

In _Jesus and the Language of the Kingdom_, Norman Perrin extends the new hermeneutic's view of language by arguing that the Kingdom should be regarded as a symbol. Previous discussions, such as Bultmann's, he says, mistakenly treated the Kingdom as a concept and left many unanswerable questions. For example, the debate whether Jesus considered the Kingdom to be present, future, or both, falsely assumed that the Kingdom was a fixed idea. To correct this false assumption Perrin, following Wheelwright and Ricoeur, uses the distinction between a "steno-symbol" and a "tensive symbol" to develop his understanding of the Kingdom. In a "steno-symbol" there is a one-to-one correspondence between the symbol and its referent, so that its meaning tends to be exhausted in its literal application. For Ricoeur (and Jung) this is called a sign, and only if the Kingdom were a sign, which Perrin denies, would it be correct to interpret it as a concept. Bultmann regards Jesus' apocalyptic expectations as erroneous, because he assumes that Kingdom is a steno-symbol that refers to a definite historical moment in which the "Son of Man" is to appear to end the world.11 A "tensive symbol," which Perrin claims the Kingdom is, cannot be exhausted by its initial referent, however, for it is open to polyvalent interpretation. For Ricoeur (and Jung) this is a true symbol whose meaning is not expressible in any better form.

Two significant objections to Perrin's usage have been raised by reviewers of his book. First, John Dominic Crossan disputes the adequacy of the steno-symbol/tensive symbol distinction. He argues that any sign/symbol is intrinsically polyvalent and that none is "so banal and stenographic that an artist or a mythmaker cannot rouse it into shattering power."12 Instead of contrasting a sign to a symbol, Crossan prefers to distinguish between sign/symbol and interpretation. Such a distinction, he believes, takes into account the open-ended richness of signs/symbols as compared to the univocal interpretations of even "strong" critics. Crossan's criticism of Perrin's usage, and by implication also that of Wheelwright and Ricoeur, is also applicable to Jung, who wishes to differentiate sign from symbol. Yet, as we shall see, Crossan's clarification is readily acceptable to Jung.

For Jung, a sign is an analogue, token, or abbreviated designation for a known thing, such as a badge worn by personnel to indicate their official status. A symbol, on the other hand, "is the best and highest expression of something divined but not yet known to the observer."13 A symbol may be either social or individual. A symbol with social significance touches upon a common factor that reaches into the depths of many persons. Such symbols organize the conscious and unconscious factors that form the basis of culture and provide the main imagery for individual self-understanding. The more universal the psychic material evoked by the symbol, the more compelling it is for the culture. An individual symbol functions for the single person analogously to the social symbol for the group. While certain images may be alluring for only one psyche, they are "alive" when they characterize something vital for a person that cannot be expressed in any better way.

Whether an image is regarded as a sign or a symbol, says Jung, "depends chiefly on the <u>attitude</u> of the observing consciousness; for instance, on whether it regards a given fact not merely as such but also as an expression for something unknown."14 While Jung concedes that there are some images whose symbolic power manifests itself spontaneously and does not depend merely upon the observer's consciousness,15 nevertheless, different interpreters may discover different meanings in the same symbol. To retain the importance of the standpoint of the interpreter in the symbolic process, Crossan's contrast of polyvalent sign/symbol to univocal interpretation is helpful.

Dan O. Via, Jr., raises a second concern about terminology in Perrin's work.16 He questions whether the designation "symbol" for the Kingdom of God is accurate. Via points out that Wheelwright and Ricoeur, upon whom Perrin depends, require a symbol to have a literal meaning that points to its figurative one. While "Kingdom" has a literal meaning, what literal meaning, asks Via pointedly, can the "Kingdom of God" have? The absence of any literal referent leads Via to conclude that the Kingdom of God is not a symbol, but a metaphor. Structurally, metaphor differs from symbol, since the former "presupposes a literal interpretation which is destroyed,"17 while the latter retains some literal significance. Symbol and metaphor are clearly different terms for Ricoeur, so that his numerous references to the Kingdom of God as a symbol,18 as Via notes, leave Ricoeur (and Perrin) in terminological self-contradiction. As a metaphor the Kingdom of God elicits a variety of discourses from Jesus--exhortation, proverb, and parable--to disclose its polyvalence.

Jung never makes a careful distinction between

symbol and metaphor; he tends to use them interchangeably. Usually, he prefers to describe the emergence of archetypal content into consciousness as the formation of symbols. But he also says that such content "expresses itself, first and foremost, in metaphors."19 In one place, where he is critical of those who interpret sexual images literally, Jung speaks positively of taking "sexual metaphors as symbols for something unknown."20 While Jung's terminology may lack precision, his main concern is to preserve the figurative significance of language, whether symbolic or metaphoric, and to develop a concomitant method of interpretation.

In contrast to Freud, who thinks that dream language deliberately hides its latent meaning and so requires a causal-reductive interpretation (Ricoeur's hermeneutics of suspicion), Jung develops the method of amplification to discover the meaning of a dream that emerges in the formation of its imagery (Ricoeur's hermeneutics of retrieval). Jung does not attempt to explain dream imagery by reducing it to contents or experiences concealed behind the symbols or metaphors. Rather, a dream's meaning is found by amplifying its symbols and metaphors with related symbols and metaphors to elicit a dream's polyvalence. While his terminology is often inconsistent, Jung's description of the nature and function of symbols/metaphors is useful to interpreters of biblical imagery.

As a metaphor, the Kingdom does not refer to an apocalyptic event in the future that would exhaust its significance. Rather, as Perrin suggests, the Kingdom evokes a range of meanings that includes the myth of god's activity in Israel's history and a decisive final act of God in which the world will be reconciled. The tension between "Kingdom" and "God" in the metaphor places the temporal under the impact of the ultimate, and ushers a person into a pattern that is rooted in the past, yet extends into the future. As a metaphor the meaning of the kingdom does not lie in Jesus' self-understanding, which he projected into apocalyptic imagery. Rather, it is because Jesus was incorporated into that which the Kingdom signifies that his existential self-understanding emerged. Since this self-understanding, says Perrin, is basically what Bultmann described it as, the emphasis on the Kingdom as metaphor arrives at Bultmann's position "by a more defensible hermeneutical method."21

Utilizing Perrin's modification of Bultmann's hermeneutics, we may claim that the eschatological thrust of Jesus' proclamation: (1) guarantees the autonomy of the Kingdom; (2) places a person in a crisis in which a new self-undestanding emerges; and (3) reveals that one's true self is always an unfinished project, since a metaphor lives beyond sheer immediacy and directs one into its multivalency.

While Jung did not specifically wrestle with the eschatological dimension of Jesus' proclamation, his understanding of symbolic language would support Bultmann's insistence on the Kingdom's autonomy. Jung says:

> It is not we who invent myth, rather it speaks to us as a Word of God. The word of God comes to us, and we have no way of distinguishing whether and to what extent it is different from God. There is nothing about this Word that could not be considered known and human, except for the manner in which it confronts us spontaneously and places obligations upon us. It is not affected by the arbitrary operation of our will. We cannot explain an inspiration. Our chief feeling about it is that it is not the result of our own ratiocinations, but that it came to us from elsewhere.22

This statement is packed with complicated issues, not the least of which is what Jung means by God! But for our purpose, it is enough to indicate that he considers consciousness only a small, albeit a vital, aspect of our totality, and, since figurative language contains unconscious as well as conscious contents, its origin points to autonomous factors uncontrollable by the will. Dreams, for example, which employ symbols/metaphors are not created by consciousness but endured. For Jung the autonomy of symbolic language results from the independence of the unconscious from the ego. Yet Bultmann would argue for the autonomy of the Kingdom over against both the unconscious and consciousness, so that Jung's claim that myth "is the revelation of divine life in man" would be unacceptable to him.23 This difference may not be as great as it first seems, however.

Jung continually insists that his statements about God are merely descriptions of observable psychic phenomena and are not ontological or theological claims. To speak of the divine life in humans is not necessarily to claim that God is reducible to an immanence in the soul. On the other hand, by the autonomy of the Kingdom Bultmann does not mean that God can be understood apart form human experience. To speak of God is, according to him, to speak of one's own self-understanding. Jung does not deny the possibility that God is _extra_ _nos_; Bultmann does not deny that God-talk describes human experience. Both Jung and Bultmann agree that speech about God is in some sense speech about the self. The eschatology of the Kingdom and the autonomy of symbolic language are two ways to preserve the "otherness" of religious claims.

Important differences between Jung and Bultmann still remain, however. For one thing, Jung's understanding of symbolic language is closer to Perrin's views than to Bultmann's, and, secondly, Bultmann's rejection of any relation between human development and the finality of the Kingdom is clearly contrary to Jung's express statements. Is there any way to reconcile the "otherness" of the Kingdom with psychological development? While Bultmann denies such a possibility, Perrin points a way toward resolution.

In his Presidential Address to the meeting of the Society of Biblical Literature in 1973, Perrin reaches the point where he demonstrates that the Kingdom is a "tensive symbol" in the teaching of Jesus and yet states that the hermeneutical task is incomplete. I quote him at length.

> What does such a symbol _do_? What kind of a response does the use of such a symbol _evoke_? I am asking that question not so much in the sense of historical criticism—what _did_ it do or evoke in terms of the first century—as in the sense of hermeneutics—what _does_ it do or evoke in terms of the twentieth century? But I ask that question only to have to admit that I have as yet no firm answer to it. I could, of course, echo Paul Ricoeur and say that the symbol gives rise to thought, that the function of a true or tensive symbol is to

tease the mind into ever new evocations of meanings. This is a valid and important insight, but, even as I utter it, I am aware that I am not so much enunciating a principle as announcing a program. One of the tasks to which I believe we have to commit ourselves as biblical scholars is the investigation of the function or evocative power of biblical symbols. This will, of course, take us into the field of psychology and the psychological processes of human understanding, but then one of the characteristics of the contemporary situation in biblical scholarship is that it challenges us to do things that we have not done before.24

By stressing the evocative power of metaphor, we can avoid the pitfall of Jung's identification of the Kingdom with an inner process and retain the Kingdom's autonomy. While Bultmann correctly argues that the Kingdom is an event that proceeds without human help or comprehension, such autonomy does not eliminate the evocative power of a metaphor to initiate a response within the self. The autonomy of the Kingdom is preserved by its eschatological dimension, and a proper interpretation of the Kingdom demands that one safeguard this aspect; yet the coming of the Kingdom into one's self-understanding evokes a response within one's psyche as does any emerging metaphor. Jung's grasp of the effects of a symbol/metaphor upon a person's development helps clarify this point.

The purpose of a symbol, says Jung, is to mediate between the known and the unknown. It tends to dissolve the tension of opposites that exists within a person to produce "a new, uniting function that transcends them."25 Such a uniting symbol may dominate one's whole attitude, canalizing one's energies into an adventure of the spirit. It may point backwards to the past, anticipate the future, reveal the present, or do all three simultaneously. Symbols not only urge conscious and unconscious aspects of the self to unite, but they contain within themselves a vision of the goal of individuation. If all of Jesus' teaching and activity are amplifications of the metaphor "Kingdom of God," then an interpretation of Jesus' proclamation, following Jung's claims, will need to demonstrate that the

Kingdom as a "living metaphor" heals splits within a person who participates in its meaning and also lures one toward wholeness.

The healing power of the Kingdom is evident in Luke 11:20, where Jesus says,"But if it is by the finger of God that I cast out demons then the kingdom has come upon you." This saying assumes that the world is pervaded by powers over which humans have no control and which often take possession of individuals. Those exorcised experienced the uniting power of the Kingdom to overcome the splits within. Such healing testifies to the reigning of God in human existence, so that restoration to wholeness and participation in the Kingdom go hand in hand.

To demonstrate more clearly, however, what Jesus' proclamation psychologically evokes, we will examine some of Jesus' parables. The parables are chosen for two reasons. First, they are widely accepted as authentic teachings of Jesus, and second, they have been subjected recently to intensive scholarly study. According to James Robinson, Perrin, and Crossan, among others, parables are actualizations of God's kingly reign in narrative. If their purpose is to lead hearers into a confrontation with his or her self-understanding, as these scholars claim, what are the implications of this confrontation for the development of wholeness?

Robinson argues that Jesus' parables, understood as God's happening, confront the structure of reality held by those in "the Establishment," who manifest the idolatrous tendency of the homo religiosus to equate actualized meaning with ultimacy.26 Perrin claims that the parables reveal God as the one who shatters the everyday world of experience and who leaves "no hint of a structured supportive community."27 Crossan describes, rather persuasively, how Jesus' parables manifest the advent, reversal, and action of the Kingdom, where reversal radically challenges a listener to abandon secured values in order to give God room to be God.28 The use of Jungian categories to interpret the psychological significance of the parables expands upon and modifies those attempts to state what happens when one participates in the meaning of Jesus' parables. The method employed will be to concentrate upon the types and fates of the characters in the parables to demonstrate that two of the structural components of the psyche conceived by

Jung--persona and shadow--help clarify what Robinson, Perrin, and Crossan call, in their different ways, a structural reversal of self-understanding.

According to Jung, the persona is the universal drive in the structure of the psyche that enables a person to adapt to the collective values of a culture. The development of one's persona occurs in reaction to a number of different influences. In childhood one learns to adjust to parental expectations, in school one is taught dominant cultural values through exposure to literature, art, history, moral codes, and other embodiments of learning, and at work one learns to conform to an employer's standards. As Jungian analyst Jolande Jacobi says, "the formation of a persona is then an important part of our education, for it regulates the relation between people and makes harmonious contact possible."29 The more one meets the public, the more necessary it becomes to have a flexible, yet stable, persona.

In a healthy individual, the persona acts as a shield against the fear of new situations, or external demands, by providing the person with an acceptable facade behind which to hide his or her private, inner life. Depending upon what circumstance demands, one's persona may change. One does not usually act the same at play as at work, in the intimacy of a family, or in large public gatherings. One may alternately wear a mask that is romantic or classic, shy or aggressive, libertine or rigidly formal. The Pharisees, for example, have been stereotyped into rigidly formal persona types in the New Testament. But whatever shape one's mask may take, without a persona one would stand "naked," and therefore vulnerable, before the world. Since the persona serves as a covering for the inner self, it is represented in dreams and literature by such images as clothes, veils, shields, tools or equipment of a trade or profession, automobiles, awards, uniforms, architectural styles, or any other cultural status symbol.

The parable of the wedding garment (Matt. 22:11-14), as the article of clothing suggests, concerns the fate of a character whose persona is not suited to the situation. Probably the Matthean author is responsible for attaching this parable to the parable of the great supper and for adding verses 13-14, which change the parable into an allegory that warns against complacency within the church. On the assumption that the introductions to the two parables of the great supper and the wedding garment were similar, the original form of the latter may be something like the following:

> The Kingdom of heaven is like a king who made a wedding for his son. And the wedding hall was filled with guests. But when the king came in to see the guests, he found there a man who had no wedding garment; and he said to him, "Friend how did you get in here without a wedding garment?" And he was speechless. Then the king said to his attendants, "Bind him hand and foot and throw him out."

The thrust of the parable does not overturn "the Establishment," nor does it shatter the everyday world of experience as Robinson, Perrin, and Crossan would lead us to believe. Rather, it warns against a violation of established manners and leaves a structured supportive community intact. As Via notes, the silence of the wedding guest "suggests that he had become aware of the unfittingness of his action."30 While the self-understanding of the ill-clad guest is threatened, it is unlikely that the listeners of the parable would be upset. Would not most hearers believe the social misfit got what he deserved? Without proper adaptation to the social environment, without a healthy persona, the wedding guest is excluded from the joyous celebration of the Kingdom.

While a healthy persona is essential for a person, there always lurks the danger of an overidentification with one's persona and a consequent state of inflation. A state of inflation occurs when the ego identifies with a content of the unconscious and naively assumes that it is in control of its power. An inflated ego does not move toward transformation, which leads to healing, but to self-righteousness and compulsiveness. Inflated persons may be very polite but have no depth of feeling, act respectably but lack moral sensitivity. Unlike the wedding guest, who is a social misfit, one suffering from persona identification acts habitually and mechanically in accord with social convention. This "mass man" lacks genuine individuality and is easily seduced by external demands or manipulated by those in power. A challenge against an inflated ego-pesona complex emerges from unconscious factors that are deemed inferior or immoral by collective standards but that provide necessary limits to social adaptation. These unconscious traits, which are highly valued in many parables of Jesus, comprise what Jung calls the shadow.

The shadow is used in different ways by Jung in his published writings. Sometimes he refers to those aspects of society that are not valued in collective consciousness, such as the repressed sexual attitudes of the Victorian age, the untouchables in India's traditional caste structure, or the Jews in Nazi Germany. Or the shadow is said to be all those aspects of the self that could be conscious but that are repressed because they are not compatible with ego-ideals or one's persona. Or Jung may refer to the shadow as an archetype that exists a priori and is not a result of repressed material. As we shall see, the parable of the good Samaritan exposes a shadow problem in Israelite culture, while the unjust steward suggests the importance of the shadow for individual development.

Traditionally, the good Samaritan has been viewed as an example story rather than a parable, i.e., it is regarded as a narrative that presents a model of neighborliness to be imitated. Via ardently defends treating the good Samaritan as an example story,31 while Crossan provides cogent arguments in favor of interpreting it as a parable.32 The distinction between parable and example story, argued by these two scholars, will not be developed here. Via's claim that an example story cannot be a metaphor for the Kingdom of God, however, needs to be examined.33

In what Via calls the "narrative parables," which for him are metaphors of the Kingdom of God, there is a king-master-father character who is involved in a dramatic confrontation with a son-servant-subordinate figure. Such tension in the narrative serves as a metaphor for the tension between the divine and the human. Example stories such as the good Samaritan, he insists, lack semantic distance and tension and, therefore, do not depict "a new vision of everyday existence as transcended by the surprising incursion of the transcendent."34 Example stories never get beyond a literal, one-dimensional meaning; and, consequently, they merely "remain illustrative examples of what one is to do or not to do."35 The strength of Via's position lies in his uniting form

108

and content within the parable; yet it is his interpretation that is univocal, not the parable itself. To single out the tension between characters as the sole criterion for a story of Jesus to be a metaphor for the Kingdom is too restrictive.

For example, one of the narrative parables selected by Via is the wedding garment. While there is a confrontation between a king and a guest in which the guest's self-understanding is radically questioned, it has already been suggested that most listeners of the story would find the king's action acceptable and expected. For whom, then, would the Kingdom happen if, as Via claims, the Kingdom always comes as a "surprising incursion of the transcendent" into everyday life except for the ill-clad guest? Obviously, Via does not suggest that the Kingdom happens only to characters in fiction; he means that through parabolic tension the listener finds analogous tension within his or her own existence. But such analogy from parable to listener does not occur in the wedding garment unless the audience is composed of persons who lack adequate personas and who champion attacks upon social convention. Whether or not a narrative serves as a model for the Kingdom is not restricted to its being a "parable" or "example story"; how observing consciousness responds to its language is also essential. For this reason it is fitting that Luke 10:36, a question addressed to the audience, ends the good Samaritan.

Both Via and Crossan agree that the use of the Samaritan in the story introduces novelty into the expectation of the audience. Via argues that the "narrative is a metaphor which gives a new meaning to the responsibilities of neighborliness,"[36] whereas for Crossan the "literal point of the story challenges the hearer to put together two impossible and contradictory words for the same person: 'Samaritan' (10:33) and 'neighbor' (10:36)."[37]

The desecration of the Temple between A.D. 6 and 9 by Samaritans, who threw dead bones in the sacred area, exemplifies the hostile relations between Jews and Samaritans in the first century. Even though both groups traced their descent from the patriarchs, the Jews questioned the Samaritan blood line and their worship practices, excluded them from participation in cultic rites at Jerusalem, and prohibited eating meat slaughtered for a Samaritan and using Samaritan

drinking vessels. According to rabbinic writings, the
Samaritans "have   no   law, not even the remnants of a
commandment,   and   are thus suspect and degenerate."38
The Samaritans, therefore, are regarded as enemies of
Yahwistic religion and as such represent one aspect of
the shadow of Jewish consciousness (Gentiles being
another).   This historical context provides the basis
for   understanding how Jewish listeners would be
expected to respond to the parable of the good
Samaritan.

Whether a Jerusalem Jew, to whom the story was
most likely told, identified himself with the robbed
man, as Robert Funk thinks,39 or with the hero who
turns out unexpectedly to be a Samaritan, as Robert
Tannehill claims,40 he would be confronted with a
disturbing decision: to accept the Samaritan, the
hated enemy, as one who loves and cares.   Such
approval of the cultural shadow would usher a hearer
into a reversal of values that judges previous
self-understanding.   The   parable   of   the   good
Samaritan, as an actualization of the Kingdom,
shatters the structure of the audience's expectations
and gives positive value to one whom the collective
consciousness of Jesus' time abhorred. To love the
shadow, to accept the unacceptable aspects of society,
takes courage, for one runs the risk of being banished
or shunned by one's fellow citizens. The Kingdom,
apparently, demands such risk.

The parable of the unjust steward discloses
another facet of the shadow problem within the
teaching of Jesus, but before discussing that parable,
further elabortion of the notion of shadow within
Jungian psychology is needed. We need to grasp what
positive function the shadow performs within the
structure of the individual psyche and why its
integration into consciousness is essential for
wholeness.

In the development of the ego-persona complex,
experiences of the world that do not appear to
correspond to one's own needs or ideals, or which are
incompatible with collective values and the need for
adaptation, are usually repressed.   One cannot be
conscious of everything, so that some things which
could be conscious are banished from awareness. These
banished feelings, thoughts, sensations, and
intuitions comprise what Jung calls the personal
unconscious and form an autonomous personality

110

compensatory to consciousness. The "inner brother or sister" is usually projected onto disliked persons who bear our shadow for us. To the extent that we do not recognize our own negative traits, a part of our personality that contains the seeds of our individuality is split off. If we never acknowledge our shadow, we become "mass men" mechanically accepting collectivist trends. The journey toward wholeness or individuation, Jung insists, requires the acceptance of our shadow and its integration into consciousness.

The parable of the unjust steward (Luke 16:1-9) depicts a character, aptly described as a picaresque type by Via,41 who successfully cheats his master. The apparent immorality of this parable created problems for the early church, so that verses 8b-9 were added to the parable to soften its impact. C. H. Dodd says about these verses, "We can almost see here notes for the three separate sermons on the parable as text."42 Some modern interpreters, also disturbed by the story, seek to explain away the steward's behavior.43 But the picaresque or trickster figure cannot be forced into the mold of collective values. Rather, he lives by his wits and cunning.

In the parable the steward is fired for squandering his master's property and is faced with the prospect of digging or begging for his survival, neither of which appeals to him. Alone with himself he decides what to do to gain favor with his master's debtors and to secure his financial future: he falsifies his accounts so that the debtors pay less. If the first half of verse 8 is the original ending of the parable, then his employer admires his clever, albeit dishonest, wisdom. If the parable ends with verse 7, then the steward's crime goes undetected. In either case the parable supports the steward's action.

What would happen to a person "parabled" by this story? Certainly, a structural reversal of a listener's expectations occurs. While there may be comic relief, sometimes even catharsis, in the antics of a trickster, usually the victims of impish pranks or malicious actions take revenge on the piccaro.44 It is doubtful that anyone in the audience expected the steward's success. Yet the positive evaluation given the trickster may be compared to one's personal shadow, which is compensatory to consciousness and autonomous. As long as the shadow remains unconscious, it acts compulsively and is the cause of much individual suffering. The shadow, while seemingly negative, actually hides meaningful contents, and its acceptance is the first step in coming to terms with the unconscious. By making one's shadow-trickster side conscious, a person assimilates and transforms his or her fascination with evil and is liberated from unconscious compulsion. Such liberation is essential for individuation. The parable of the unjust steward invites one to participate in the Kingdom by recognizing the cleverness of the steward, as does the master in verse 8, even though his behavior might offend one's moral assumptions.

The importance of both persona and shadow may be seen in the parable of the prodigal son (Luke 15:11-32), but before demonstrating that position let us look at the Jungian reading of the parable given by Via. Employing the model of the Self-ego axis developed by Jungian analyst Edward Edinger, Via interprets the prodigal as the ego, the elder brother as the prodigal's shadow, and the father as the Self.45 The difficulty with this interesting interpretation, even if one could accept Via's psychological designations of each character, is the assumption that each character is a personification of a single psychic component, a procedure more suited to allegory. It seems methodologically more sound to regard each character as having an ego-complex and to decide what kind of personality is exhibited by each one's actions. Such a method takes into account the "rugged realism" of parabolic language.46

In relation to the conscious values of his family, the prodigal lives out the shadow side of his culture and ends up wasting his inheritance, cavorting with harlots, and becoming destitute. At the nadir of despair he is no better than a hated Gentile, tending hogs and, consequently, no longer shaped by the family's persona. When he becomes conscious of the disastrous consequences of an uncritical descent into the shadow, however, he returns home and is welcomed back into the supportive structure of the family: the father orders a robe, shoes, and the family ring to be put on his wayward and vulnerable son. The father's action restores value to a son who gains a new persona after his descent into, and subsequent emergence out of, the shadow.

The elder brother, on the other hand, typifies one whose ego is overidentified with collective values and exhibits a rigid persona: he is the always dutiful son. Naturally, he is disturbed by his father's approval of his independent brother and of the celebration given for him. His anger and jealousy, however, are the stirrings of the shadow, which if integrated could enable the brother to break out of his collective posture and discover his own individuality. While the elder brother is not enjoying the merriment, he, too, is valued by the father who says, "All that is mine is yours."

Once again a listener's expectations may meet with surprise, since the prodigal is celebrating a restoration to family honor, while the dutiful son goes seemingly unrewarded. But the reversal is mild in comparison with the good Samaritan and the unjust steward, for the return of a "lost" or "dead" son would appeal to a basic desire for reconciliation within a family and for unity within one's own psyche.47 Such a reunion presents a vision of the goal of the Kingdom. The parable, through the action of the father, supports both persona and shadow. While the integration of the two is evident in the father, the process has only begun for the elder brother.

The parables of Jesus demonstrate the need both to adapt to collective consciousness and to challenge established values by integrating the shadow. Only in the latter case may we speak of a structural reversal of self-understanding. To overemphasize dramatic reversal of ordinary expectations is to undermine the place of adaptation and continuity in everyday experience. William Beardslee has demonstrated that the bulk of synoptic proverbs attributable to Jesus, and to wisdom literature in general, champions conventional consciousness and allows one to make a continuous whole out of one's existence. Only when a firm base in everydayness is formed within one's ego-complex is it valuable to confront a person with either a parable or a proverb whose purpose is "to jolt the hearer into a new insight."48 Some parables do jolt one's expectations, as Crossan more than any other interpreter makes clear. The thrust of these parables is to esteem traits deemed inferior, to invite love of the seemingly unlovable, and to expand, rather than simply reverse, the structure of consciousness.

113

The evocative power of the Kingdom, whether embodied in exorcism, parable, or wisdom saying, awakens a depth in the psyche that might otherwise remain dormant. It places a person in self and world examination, as Bultmann claims. But his claim that such an examination excludes a possible development in one's inner life ignores the capacity of a metaphor both to tease the mind into ever new meanings and to lure a person into a quest for greater and greater self-understanding. The eschatological thrust of the Kingdom as an autonomous, polyvalent metaphor evokes a permanent challenge to one's imagined self-sufficiency. While the Kingdom is not an inner process within the psyche, its incarnation in the proclamation of Jesus evokes a pattern of development that has striking resemblance to what Jung calls individuation.

1. Rudolf Bultmann, _Jesus and the Word_, trans. Louise Pettibone Smith and Erminine Huntress Latero (New York: Charles Scribner's Sons, 1958), p. 38.

2. _Ibid._, p. 47.

3. C. G. Jung, _Two Essays on Analytical Psychology_, trans. R. F. C. Hull, _Collected Works_, Vol. 7 (Princeton: Princeton University Press), p. 226.

4. _Ibid._

5. C. G. Jung, _Psychology and Alchemy_, trans. R. F. C. Hull, _Collected Works_, Vol. 12 (Princeton: Princeton University Press, 1974), p. 8.

6. C. G. Jung, _Aion_, trans. R. F. C. Hull, _Collected Works_, Vol. 9,ii, 2nd ed., (Princeton: Princeton University Press, 1968), p. 37, n. 4.

7. Rudolf Bultmann, _Kerygma and Myth_, ed. by Hans Werner Bartsch, trans. Reginald H. Fuller (New York: Harper and Brothers, 1961), p. 10.

8. _Jesus and the Word_, p. 52.

9. Rudolf Bultmann, _Glauben and Verstehen_, Vol. 3 (Tubingen, J. C. B. Mohr [Paul Siebeck], 1960), p. 88.

10. _Jesus and the Word_, p. 36.

11. There are a number of scholars who deny the authenticity of the Son of Man sayings attributed to Jesus in the New Testament. The accuracy of Bultmann's historical judgment in this matter, however, is not essential to the argument under discussion.

12. John Dominic Crossan, "Literary Criticism and Biblical Hermeneutics," _Journal of Religion_, 51, p. 78.

13. C. G. Jung, Psychological Types, trans. R. F. C. Hull, Collected Works, Vol. 6 (Princeton: Princeton University Press, 1971), p. 474.

14. Ibid., p. 475.

15. Ibid., p. 476.

16. Dan O. Via, Jr., "Kingdom and Parable: The Search for a New Grasp of Symbol, Metaphor, and Myth," Interpretation, 31, pp. 181-83.

17. Paul Ricoeur, "Biblical Hermeneutics," Semeia, 4, p. 78.

18. Ibid., pp. 99-101; 133f.

19. C. G. Jung, The Archetypes and the Collective Unconscious, trans. R. F. C. Hull, Collected Works, Vol. 9,i (Princeton: Princeton University Press, 1975), p. 157.

20. C. G. Jung, The Structure and Dynamics of the Psyche, trans. R. F. C. Hull, Collected Works, Vol. 8 (Princeton: Princeton University Press, 1972), p. 264.

21. Norman Perrin, Jesus and the Language of the Kingdom (Philadelphia: Fortress, 1976), p. 264.

22. C. G. Jung, Memories, Dreams, Reflections, ed. Aniela Jaffe, trans. Richard and Clara Winston (New York: Vintage Books, 1961), p. 340.

23. Ibid.

24. Norman Perrin, "Eschatology and Hermeneutics: Reflections on Method in the Interpretation of the New Testament," Journal of Biblical Literature, 93, p. 13.

25. Psychological Types, p. 479.

26. James M. Robinson, "Jesus' Parables as God Happening," in Jesus and the Historian, ed. F. Thomas Trotter (Philadelphia: Westminster Press, 1968), p. 146.

27. Jesus and the Language of the Kingdom, p. 199.

28. John Dominic Crossan, _In Parables_ (New York: Harper and Row, 1973), passim and _The Dark Interval_ (Niles, Illinois: Argus Communications, 1975), p. 121.

29. Jolande Jacobi, _Masks of the Soul_, trans. Ean Begg (Grand Rapids: William B. Eerdmans, 1976), p. 38.

30. Dan O. Via, Jr., _The Parables_ (Philadelphia: Fortress, 1967), p. 130.

31. Dan O. Via, Jr., "Parable and Example Story: A Literary-Structuralist Approach," _Semeia_, 1, p. 113.

32. John Dominic Crossan, "The Good Samaritan: Towards a Generic Definition of Parable," _Semeia_, 2, pp. 82-112.

33. _Semeia_, 1, p. 119.

34. _Ibid._, p. 118.

35. _Ibid._, p. 119.

36. _Ibid_.

37. _In Parables_, p. 64.

38. Joachim Jeremias, "Samareia, Samarites, Samaritis," _Theological Dictionary of the New Testament_, Vol. 7, ed. Gerhard Kittle and Gerhard Friedrich, trans. Geoffrey W. Bromiley (Grand Rapids: William B. Eerdmans, 1971), p. 91.

39. Robert Funk, "The Good Samaritan as Metaphor," _Semeia_, 2, pp. 74-81.

40. Cited by Perrin in _Jesus and the Language of the Kingdom_, p. 178.

41. _The Parables_, pp. 159f.

42. C. H. Dodd, _The Parables of the Kingdom_ (London: Fontana Books, 1951), p. 26.

43. T. W. Manson, _The Sayings of Jesus_ (London: SCM Press, 1975), pp. 290-93.

117

44. C. G. Jung, Collected Works, 9,i, pp. 255-72.

45. Dan O. Via, Jr., "The Prodigal Son: A Jungian Reading," Semeia, 9, pp. 21-43.

46. Ernest Cadman Colwell, Jesus and the Gospel (Oxford: Oxford University Press, 1963), pp. 33-35.

47. Mary Ann Tolbert, Perspectives on the Parables (Philadelphia: Fortress, 1979), pp. 102f.

48. William A. Beardslee, "Use of the Proverb in the Synoptic Gospels," Interpretation, 24, p. 61.

CHAPTER 7

A JUNGIAN APPROACH TO THE JŌDOSHINSHŪ

CONCEPT OF THE "WICKED"

Mokusen Miyuki

Shinran (1173-1262 A.D.), the founder of Jōdoshinshū Buddhism in Kamakura Japan, is revolutionary in his conviction that "If even the virtuous can attain rebirth (in the Pure Land), how much more so the wicked!"1 I will demonstrate that what Shinran means by the "wicked" corresponds to what C. G. Jung designates as the shadow and that, accordingly, the rebirth of the "wicked" is parallel to shadow integration.

Jung observes that the shadow, being the dark side of the personality, is rejected by the ego and is driven into the unconscious. The result is a psychic imbalance due to the cleavage thus created between conscious and unconscious. Therefore, the conscious acceptance of the shadow, or the "wicked" within, helps the individual enlarge and strengthen ego-consciousness through the integration of the alienated or disowned part of oneself. Shadow integration, according to Jung, designates a dialectical process of the confrontation of the ego, the center of conscious personality, with the unconscious to make a split psyche a whole. Such a process Jung calls "individuation," whereby "a person becomes a psychological 'individual,' that is, a separate, invisible unity or 'whole'."2

Jung also designates individuation as "becoming

one's own self" as well as "self-realization."3 The German term translated as "self-realization" is Selbstverwirklichung, which, to my understanding, indicates the psychological urge of the Self to realize itself consciously--the Self being the regulating center and the whole circumference of both the conscious and unconscious psyche.4 This point is clarified by Edward F. Edinger when he states: "Individuation seems to be the innate urge of life (the Self) to realize itself consciously. The transpersonal life energy in the process of self-unfolding uses human consciousness, a product of itself, as an instrument for its own self realization."5 Shinran's seemingly amoral conviction concerning the rebirth of the "wicked" into the Pure Land, then, may be viewed psychologically as a Buddhist example of shadow integration, as the Self's manifesting itself in consciousness.

Shinran's insight that the realization of the "wicked" within is paradoxicaly the very thing which liberates oneself may have occurred to him while he was examining the legend of Ajātaśatru, the King of Magadha in ancient India.6 He was concerned with this legend for much of his life, perhaps because of his own position as an exile within his own society.7 He became an exile at the age of thirty-five when he was punished for the religious practice of the Nembutsu, or the mental and/or verbal recitation of Amida's name.8 Thereafter, Shinran thought of himself as being "neither monk nor layman"; he called himself "gutoku," or "stupid (gu) and bald-headed (toku)," which I maintain connotes someone who is a wicked outcast from both the secular and religious community.9

I. The Legend of Ajātaśatru

The legend of Ajātaśatru echoes the tragedy of Oedipus. Ajātaśatru kills his father, King Bimbisāra, in order to usurp the throne. This tragedy took place when Ajātaśatru discovered the past karmic secret of his birth from Devadatta. Devadatta, a rival cousin of the Buddha, is said to have harbored the idea of taking Buddha's place as the leader of the Order.10 When the Buddha refused his request, Devadatta was angered. He goes to Ajātaśatru, whose patronage and admiration he had enjoyed, with the plan to kill the Buddha and have Ajātaśatru kill his father Bimbisāra.

Devadatta tells Ajātaśatru the story of his birth. Bimbisāra wanted a son for years. He consulted a seer who said that a certain hermit would die three years hence and reincarnate as Bimbisāra's heir. The King, being impatient, sent someone to murder the hermit to hasten the birth of a heir. As prophesied, the Queen, Vaidehi, became pregnant. Both King and Queen greatly rejoiced; however, when Bimbisāra was told by another seer that his son would eventually kill him when he grew up, the King's joy was turned into great fear. The King, thereupon, ordered the Queen to give birth to the child in a tower, so that he could kill the infant by dropping him onto the ground. The infant, however, survived the fall; he only broke one of his little fingers. For this reason, people called this child Balaruci, "the broken finger," or "Ajātaśatru, the grudge-not-yet-born."

Ajātaśatru was troubled by Devadatta's story and inquired of a minister who confirmed its truth. Enraged, Ajātaśatru imprisoned his father with the intention to starve him to death. Learning of her son's plot, the Queen Vaidehi brought food and drink secretively to her husband, King Bimbisāra. When Ajātaśatru discovered his mother's action, he became so outraged that he planned to kill her, too. Two ministers, Jīvaka and Candraprabha, cautioned him that matricide is an act of candāla and that he would become a despised outcast who would be put to death.11 Afraid of such a fate, Ajātaśatru changed his mind and merely confined his mother to a remote room in the palace.12

After the King's death, Ajātaśatru's remorse grew; foul smelling sores broke out all over his body. He realized that his agony was the karmic result of patricide and that he was going to fall into hell. His mother, now freed from her imprisonment, applied various medicines to cure his bodily sores in vain. His six ministers advised him to consult their respective teachers whose doctrine of karma might alleviate his agony and fear of going to hell. But Jīvaka, a physician and one of the ministers, encouraged Ajātaśatru to see the Buddha, "the Great Physician," who had the power to "cure" his physical and spiritual pain. As the King was deciding what to do, he heard a voice from the sky also encouraging him to see the Buddha. Trembling with great fear, the King asked who was speaking to him. When the voice said that it was his father, Ajātaśatru fell to the ground and his agony intensified. His bodily sores became more putrescent and smelled increasingly foul.

Foreseeing Ajātaśatru's impending visit to seek his guidance, the Buddha declared that he would not enter nirvāna before liberating Ajātaśatru. When Ajātaśatru fell to the ground upon hearing his father's voice, the Buddha entered the samādhi called "moon loving" to emit light to cool off and heal Ajātaśatru's bodily sores. Ajātaśatru, astonished by this miraculous cure of his sores, is told by Jīvaka that the cure was the work of the Buddha. Jīvaka compared the Buddha's concern to heal dreadful karmic offenders like Ajātaśatru with the compassion of a mother with seven children whose thoughts are constantly directed toward her sick child rather than her healthy six children. Greatly impressed with Jīvaka's words, Ajātaśatru decided to go to the Buddha to seek guidance.

The Buddha taught the King the great importance of remorse and repentance in the recognition of his heinous patricidal karma. Then, he pointed out that Bimbisāra was destined karmically to be killed by his own son for killing the innocent hermit. Furthermore, he told Ajātaśatru that his patricide was committed not while he was of "genuine" ("sane") mind, but while he was deluded ("insane") by his greed for the throne quickened by Devadatta's instigation. The Buddha concluded that, upon being awakened, Ajātaśatru would realize that a crime committed in a deluded state does not exist. Being taught thus, Ajātaśatru experienced the awakening of his genuine mind, or bodhi-citta, by realizing that his crime of patricide was karmically preordained. The awakening of bodhi-citta was so utterly incomprehensible to him that he referred to it as "receiving the realization of the Entrusting Mind/Heart Having No Root Within."13

II.   A Jungian Interpretation of the Legend of Ajātaśatru

The legend of Ajātaśatru illuminates the doctrine of karma. The awakening of bodhi-citta occurs when Ajātaśatru, through the Buddha's guidance, realizes that his patricidal karma, entangled with his parents' infanticidal karma, originated in a deluded mind which was in turn conditioned by greed, or attachment to the throne. The process of becoming conscious of this

122

karmic drama is a Buddhist equivalent to individuation, where the ego, represented by Ajātaśatru, dialectically confronts_ unconscious contents, represented by Devadatta, Jivaka, and the Buddha. These characters constitute what Jung calls "archetypes": they are archetypes that have become accessible to the ego as the ego journeys further into the depths of the psyche.

Jung explains archetypes in conjunction with karma, which he regards as "a sort of psychic theory of heredity based on the hypothesis of reincarnation."14 What he means by "psychic heredity" is "the universal disposition" of the psyche which are forms, or categories, of the imagination, analogous to Plato's forms (eidola). Being categories of the imagination, these forms are "always in essence visual" and "always and everywhere present."15 Jung states, these:

> forms must, from the outset, have the character of images and moreover of typical images, which is why, following St. Augustine, I call them 'archetypes.' Comparative religion and mythology are rich mines of archetypes, and so is the psychology of dreams and psychoses.16

The central archetype as the regulating core of the entire psyche is the archetype of the Self. In the legend, the Self is represented by the image of the Buddha who is fully awakened to the karmic nexus and whose karmic omniscience forms a dynamic continuum with compassion. For, the Buddha foresaw Ajātaśatru's visit and postponed his entrance into nirvāna for the sake of Ajātaśatru. Psychologically speaking, then, Ajātaśatru's karmic life is an inner drama impelled and carried out by the Buddha, or the Self, unknown to the consciousness of Ajātaśatru, or ego. This unconscious urging is clearly indicated by Ajātaśatru's use of the expression "utterly incomprehensible" when he experiences the awakening of Bodhi-citta as "receiving the realization of the Entrusting Mind/Heart Having No Root Within."

The tragedy of Ajātaśatru's patricide takes place at the instigation of Devadatta. Devadatta is the mortal rival of the Buddha and, as such, functions as the dark side of the Buddha. For Jung, the Self is the paradoxical unity in which all the opposites are united such as good/evil, light/darkness, or conscious/unconscious; consequently, without integration of "evil," there is no realization of totality. As Jung states, whenever the archetype of the self predominates, the inevitable psychological consequence is a state of conflict and man "must suffer from the opposite of his intention for the sake of completeness.17"

Moreover, according to Jung,

> the archetypes have, when they appear, a distinctly numinous character which can only be described as 'spiritual,' if 'magical' is too strong a word. . . . It can be healing or destructive, but never indifferent, provided of course that it has attained a certain degree of clarity.18

In this vein, we can take diabolical Devadatta as Ajātaśatru's archetypal shadow, representing the powerful, destructive aspect of the archetype of the Self.

In confronting the numinosity of the archetypal shadow, the ego is greatly endangered, or even lost as seen in the case of a psychotic episode. The more repressed or rejected, the more archetypal the shadow becomes, being more alienated from, and unrelated to, the ego. The psychic conflict due to the cleavage thus created between conscious and unconscious results in a state of psychic unbalance. In other words, being threatened by the numinosity of the shadow, the ego's functioning is so seriously menanced that a lowering of the threshold of consciousness (abaissement du niveau mental) takes place. Jung describes such a state as a state of psychic dissociation in which "the normal checks imposed by the conscious mind" is abolished and "thus gives unlimited scope to the play of the unconscious 'dominants'."19 This description, Jung maintains, also indicates the essential characteristic of mental illness.20 This dissociation happens to Ajātaśatru when he is informed by Devadatta about the "dark" secret of his karmic past.

The devastating effects of the unprepared ego to encounter the Self is depicted in Ajātaśatru's compulsion to commit the "insane" act of matricide. The mother is the source of life; therefore, matricide symbolizes the act of severing the very root of one's being. Such an act is typical of a __candala__, the despised outcaste whose very existence is denied. The admonition of the two ministers against the act of matricide, therefore, is viewed as a manifestation of the light of conscience experienced by the ego; this will eventually be followed by an experience of intense suffering on the part of the ego.

It is maintained that the ego's failure of conscious integration of the psychic conflict could lead to somatization of the inner discord.21 This is the case of Ajātaśatru, who suffers greatly from bodily sores. Being urged by the awakened conscience, he is forced relentlessly to find the meaning of his dreadful karma of patricide and seeks to understand the doctrine of karma through various teachers. The more he listens to their teachings, the more intense his suffering and agony becomes due to his progressive awareness of the hopelessly dreadful karmic act he has committed. Thus, Ajātaśatru senses acutely the impending hell with tremendous fear and remorse.

The seventh teacher, the Buddha, is recommended to Ajātaśatru by Jīvaka. In view of the cosmic symbolism of the number seven exemplified in "seven planets," the Buddha as the seventh teacher signifies "the Great Physician" whose healing activity penetrates the universe. The Buddha as the "cosmic" healer is also seen in the image of the mother whose compassion is directed toward the sick, or "seventh," child, rather than toward the six healthy ones.

The healing process of the Self's urge continues in a more articulated manner as the ego becomes more conscious of its hopeless situation. This is symbolized in the story by the voice of Ajātaśatru's father wishing and encouraging him to see the Buddha in the midst of his absolute despair. For Ajātaśatru, this is utterly incomprehensible. Ajātaśatru, who trembles and falls to the ground, indicates the extreme severity of the ego's alienation from the Self. In this dangerous state of psychic dissociation, the ego's function is destined to be subordinated to the Self's urge to realize itself. "Ego-Self separation," to use E. F. Edinger's words, is to be followed by "ego-Self" union.21

"Ego-Self union" is a state in which the restoration of the psychic balance takes place through the healing function of the Self, which in the story is seen in the act of the Buddha who enters the "moon loving" _samadhi_ which brought about the miraculous cure of Ajātaśatru's bodily sores. Ajātaśatru now seeks the Buddha for guidance and experiences _bodhi-citta_. These experiences symbolize the subordination of the ego to the "Self-centric" functioning of the psyche and the restoration to psychic wholeness. For Ajātaśatru, this awakening of _bodhi_-_citta_ is "utterly incomprehensible," for the Self, represented by _bodhi_-_citta_, is beyond the ego's comprehension.23

In summary, the legend of Ajātaśatru can be interpreted psychologically to show that, once the innate urge of the Self takes place, the Self provides the ego with a source of energy for its development, on the one hand, while, on the other, it relentlessly imposes upon the ego the task of integrating the dark side of the psyche--the unconscious. The legend of Ajātaśatru is a Buddhist equivalent to what Jung calls Self-realization. This Jungian reading of the legend of Ajātaśatru is supported by the insights of Shinran, who struggled with his shadow integration throughout his life.

III. <u>Shinran on the Legend of Ajātaśatru</u>

The legend of Ajātaśatru is used by Shinran to support his views about the Eighteenth Vow of the Amida Buddha. Shinran considers this Vow the most essential of the forty-eight vows that the Amida Buddha established in order to create the Pure Land. It states:

> Upon my attainment of Buddhahood, should the sentient beings in the ten quarters, who have sincerity of mind/heart, who rejoice in the entrusting mind/heart, and who desire rebirth into my land, if they, while repeating my name and directing their thoughts to me up to ten times, are not to be born therein, then may I not attain Buddhahood. Excluded from this are those who commit the five grave offenses and those who slander the Right Dharma.24

This vow evidently excludes persons such as the outcast Shinran and Ajātaśatru, whose patricide is one of the five grave offenses25 and prevents their rebirth into the Pure Land. However, Shinran maintains that the exclusion made in this Vow is not to be taken literally. He interprets it to mean that, if one denies one's wrongdoing, it is impossible to be born into the Pure Land; consequently, it is essential to realize the "wickedness" within oneself and to suffer when confronted with one's fear and agony. He supports this view by relating his struggle with his own shadow to the legend of Ajātaśatru in which the Buddha extends great compassion to a man who committed one of the five grave and exclusionary karmic offenses.

When Shinran labelled himself the "stupid and bald-headed one," he indicates his profound identification with the "wicked" Ajātaśatru. The word "stupid" denotes a "wicked" being within oneself, a being that is utterly devoid of a genuine mind and is capable of committing the gravest offenses. The term "bald-headed" is purposefully used by Shinran to designate himself as a spiritually "corrupted" monk who receives ordination for personal advantage instead of enlightenment. In his awareness of himself as "stupid and bald-headed," Shinran must have felt that, if the "wicked" Ajātaśatru's liberation is a primary concern for the Buddha, then those beings who are excluded from the Amida's Vow could be in fact the primary and crucial objects to be liberated by the Vow. The liberation of the "wicked" Ajātaśatru foreseen by the Buddha foreshadows the redemption of the "stupid and bald-headed" outcast Shinran. Shinran views the tragic drama concerning Ajātaśatru as occasioned by the Buddha's desire to liberate him. Accordingly, for Shinran, those characters in the story are to be taken as "incarnated" figures who symbolize various aspects of the Buddha's compassion, as Shinran states in the Preface to his major work entitled Kyōgyōshinshō:

> Thus we see these incarnated ones' [i.e., Devadatta, Ajātaśatru, Bimbisāra, Vaidehī, etc., in the legend] benevolent spirit is to save all beings from misery and suffering and that the compassionate heart of the Bravest of the world [i.e., the Buddha] extends even to criminals of the highest degree, blasphemers of the Right Dharma, indeed, to those who are utterly devoid of any stock of merit [i.e., the icchantikas or the outcastes].26

Shinran implies in this statement that it is also the Amida Buddha's intention that Shinran become an outcast so that he could find his liberation through confronting his wickedness, or the shadow.

Summary

Shinran's conviction regarding the rebirth of the "wicked" through the Amida Buddha's Vow can be regarded psychologically as a Buddhist parallel to Jung's shadow integration as Self-realization. As shadow integration consciously enables an individual to have a meaningful life, so the conscious acceptance of the "wicked" within through the Amida Buddha's Vow leads the ego into a close and intimate relationship with the Self. The result is a more differentiated psychological life, which is the essential for a rich spiritual life.

1. The Tannishō, A Tract Deploring Heresies of Faith
   (Kyoto: Higashi Hongwanji, 1961), p. 6.

2. C. G. Jung, "Conscious, Unconscious, and
   Individuation," in The Archetypes and the
   Collective Unconscious, Collected Works
   (hereafter abridged as CW), Vol. 9, (New York:
   Pantheon Books, Inc.), p. 275.

3. C. G. Jung, Two Essays on Analytical Psychology,
   CW 7, p. 173.

4. C. G. Jung, Psychology and Alchemy, CW 12, p. 41.

5. E. F. Edinger, Ego and Archetype (Baltimore,
   Maryland: Penguin Books, Inc., 1973) p. 104.

6. In his major work entitled Kyōgyōshinshō, Shinran
   uses extensive quotations from the Mahāyāna
   Nirvāna Sūtra regarding the legend of Ajātaśatru,
   the King of Magadha in ancient India. For an
   English translation, see Gutoku Shaku Shinran,
   The Kyōgyōshinshō: The Collection of Passages
   Expounding the True Teaching, Living, Faith, and
   Realizing of the Pure Land, trans. Daisetz
   Teitaro Suzuki and edited by the Eastern Buddhist
   Society (Kyoto: Shinshu Otaniha, 1973), pp.
   140-163.

7. Akamatsu Toshihide, a noted historian in Japanese
   Buddhism, proves that shinran made extensive
   quotation from the Mahāyāna Nirvāna Sūtra in his
   Kyōgyōshinshō when he revised it in his later
   years. See Akamatsu Toshihide, Shinran (Tokyo:
   Yoshikawa Kōbundō, 1961), pp. 201-274.

8. For a Jungian discussion on the Nembutsu
   Practice, or nienfo in Chinese, see Mokusen
   Miyuki, "A Jungian Approach to the Pure Land
   Practice of Nien-fo," The Journal of Analytical
   Psychology 25:3 (July 1980), pp. 266-274.

9. For a detailed discussion on the inner meaning of

Shinran's experience of exile, see Mokusen Miyuki, "Tokujin Shinran [Shinran, Stupid and bald-headed]," _Shinrankyōgaku_ 36 (July 1980), pp. 55-72.

10. For a detailed discussion on Devadata, see Edward J. Thomas, _The History of Buddhist Thought_ (London: Kegan Paul, 1933), p. 24.

11. Candāla is "an outcast, man of the lowest and most despised of the mixed tribes (born from a 'Sūdra father and a Brāhman mother." Sir Monier Monier-Williams, _A Sanskrit-English Dictionary_ (Oxford: The Clarendon Press, 1899), p. 383.

12. This paragraph is based on the description in the _Kuan Wu-liang-shou-fo ching_. Taisho 37, No. 2753. For an English translation of this scripture, see J. Takakusu, tr., "_The Amitāyur-dhyāna-sūtra_: The Sūtra of the Meditation on Amitāyus," in _Buddhist Mahāyāna Texts_ (Sacred Books of the East, Vol. 49).

13. Ajātaśatru also depicted his experience of the awakening of _bodhi-citta_ as "a _candana_ tree which has miraculously grown in the midst of the _eranda_ forest"--the _candana_ tree, with its marvelous fragrance being able to overcome the foul smell of the _eranda_ forest, or his grave patricidal offense.

14. C. G. Jung, "On 'The Tibetan Book of the Dead'," _Psychology and Religion: West and East_, CW 11, p. 517.

15. _Ibid_.

16. _Ibid_., p. 518.

17. C. G. Jung, _Aion_, CW 9, ii, p. 69.

18. C. G. Jung, "On the Nature of the Psyche," _The Structure and Dynamics of the Psyche_, CW 8, p. 205.

19. C. G. Jung, "On 'The Tibetan Book of the Dead'," CW 11, p. 520.

20. _Ibid_.

21. This view is based on Jung's kypothesis of the "psychoid nature of the archetype." See Marion Woodman, _The Owl Was a Baker's Daughter: Obesity, Anarexia Nervosa, and the Repressed Feminine_ (Toronto: Inner City Books, 1980).

22. E. F. Edinger, _Ego and Archetype,_ p. 4.

23. It should be noted here that Ajātaśatru's or the ego's capacity to experience _bodhi-citta._ or the Self, is signified by his other name Shan-chien, meaning "seeing (_chien_) well (_shan_)."

24. The writer's translation. See also _The Kyōgyōshinshō,_ trans. D. T. Suzuki, p. 88.

25. Generally speaking, the five grave offenses are: "1) the deliberate killing of one's father, 2) the deliberate killing of one's mother, 3) the deliberate killing of an arhat, 4) to break up the harmony of the Brotherhood (_samgha_), being motivated by perverted views, 5) to bleed the Buddha-body, being intent on harming him." _The Kyōgyōshinshō,_ trans. D. T. Suzuki, p. 170. Those who commit these offenses are said to "fall instantly into the Avici [Hell] and find themselves forever unable to be released." _Ibid.,_ p. 169.

26. _Ibid.,_ p. 104.

CHAPTER 8

JUNG AND THE HISTORIAN OF RELIGION:

THE CASE OF HELLENISTIC RELIGION

Luther H. Martin

Jung's work in symbolism and comparative mythology, and especially his extensive studies in the history and phenomenology of Christianity and of the alchemical opus, should have established his contribution to the study of religion. Careful attention to Jung's work by historians of religion, however, has been sporadic, despite the appreciative acknowledgement of his work by some.1

Jung's concern with patterns or structures in man's symbolic expression, moreover, parallels attempts by historians of religion to order their morass of data. The observation of such universal structures in human culture are the basis of various typological, archetypological, and, in a broad sense, structuralist theories.2

Jung observed recurring patterns not only in man's collective expressions, such as folklore and mythology, but in individual expressions, such as dreams, as well. His early interest in archaeology3 had given way to an interest in the individual and his inner world, to an archaeology of the self. Consequently, Jung's work may be understood on two levels: his phenomenology of those patterns which recur both in collective and in individual expressions, and his psychological theory which he developed to account for these common patterns. The historian of religion need not concern himself with Jung's psychological explanations *per se*, but the very nature of his data invites a consideration of Jung's archetypology. In short, while Jung found in history what he considered to be empirical (historical and cultural) support for his psychological model, the historian of religion may well find in Jung's work an heuristic typology for organizing his historical and comparative researches.

The case of Hellenistic religion may serve as a case in point. Religion in the Hellenistic period is most often characterized by historians of religion as "syncretistic."4   This term is meant to describe the mutual influence of originally different religious traditions as they came into contact with one another under conditions of a new internationalism established by the conquests of Alexander the Great. By labeling Hellenistic religion "syncretistic," however, the historian of religion tacitly admits to a situation of historical confusion and neglects the fundamental question of the systemic unity which may belong to that world.   What are the criteria which allowed certain symbols, practices, or deities to commingle, but not others?   Such inquiry allows Hellenistic religions to be understood as religious expressions in their own right rather than as historically confused or accidental minglings of differing cultural and religious elements.

The Jungian paradigm allows the salient features of Hellenistic religiosity to be organized in integral relationship with one another. Jung understood the systemic structures of man's psyche to be projected or objectified into his perception and organization of external reality.   Consequently such "external" realities as his image of cosmology can provide an initial insight into the structure of man's symbolic world system.5

The formulaic pattern of Hellenic cosmogony is remembered for us by Euripides when he writes:

The tale is not mine, but is from my mother;
how Heaven and Earth were once one formed,
and when they had been sundered from one
another, they gave birth and brought up into
the light, all things: trees, birds,
beasts, the spawn of the sea, and race of
mortals.
                              --Frag. 484 Melanippe

133

Under the surface of the earth was the underworld while over the earth arched the heavens. A macrocosmic-microcosmic parallel was understood to exist between these differentiated realms, grounded in their primordial unity. The earth, depicted as a flat disc bouyed upon the primordial feminine waters from which it had emerged, symbolized an integrated cosmos as it reflected the mandalic perfection of the heavenly sphere. The emergent cosmic image thus refracted an inherent order. This cosmological image extended in the West from the early river civilizations of Mesopotamia and Egypt to the beginnings of Ionian speculation.

By the third century A.D., a greatly expanded image of the cosmos had emerged. Contrary to archaic cosmology, this image depicted the earth as a sphere, suspended in space, and surrounded by seven planetary spheres. The cosmos was divided into a superlunar celestial sphere of the divine and a sublunar terrestrial sphere of the profane. Thus, the primary cosmological criterion of differentiation within this new world, was the moon, the closest of the planets to the earth, and was understood with it to be of a feminine nature.6 This greatly expanded and differentiated image of the cosmos was still seen as finite, the whole contained within the spherical realm of the fixed stars.

The cosmogonic pattern of differentiation originating with the archaic image and continuing into what later was codified as the Ptolemaic cosmology is paralleled by the Jungian dynamic of individuation. In this psychological model of individual maturation, Jung understood ego development to proceed from an undifferentiated state through various stages which may be distinguished from one another according to the ego's differentiation from its feminine origin. This feminine origin initially is manifest in terms of one's personal mother. As the ego matures from its infantile attachment to its mother towards ego autonomy, the protective and nurturing embrace of the mother increasingly is experienced by the differentiating ego as a smothering grasp of death. Corresponding, consequently, to this cosmological/psychological model is the dominance of the archetypal feminine in Hellenistic mythology and in man's religious response. The development of the important Greek notion of fate into the Hellenistic period exemplifies this ruling pattern of the sovereign feminine.

The early Hellenic fates, or Moirai, corresponded collectively to a relatively undifferentiated stage of the ruling feminine archetype. Jung observed that these Moirai have both "a positive, favorable meaning or a negative, evil meaning."7 By the Hellenistic period, however, the unified ruling fates were supplanted by the rule of Tyche/Fortuna. As reported by Pliny:

> Everywhere in the whole world at every hour by all men's voices Fortune alone is invoked and named. . . . and we are so much at the mercy of chance that Chance herself, by whom God is proved uncertain, takes the place of God.
>
> --HN II, 22

Her most characteristic trait was her ambiguity or capriciousness, her double nature as positive and negative. Again, to cite Pliny:

> [Fortune is] alone accused, alone impeached, alone pondered, alone applauded, alone rebuked and visited with reproaches; deemed volitile and indeed by most men blind as well, wayward, inconstant, uncertain, fickle in her favours and favouring the unworthy. To her is debited all that is spent and credited all that is received, she alone fills both pages in the whole of mortals account.
>
> --HN II,22. 8

Unlike the Moirai, Tyche/Fortuna now is clearly differentiated into a good and evil fortune, though still embodied in a single image. The negative aspect of this ruling feminine was her capriciousness, her unreliability; luck may be either good or bad. Her beneficient aspect, on the other hand, was known as Agathe Tyche, good fortune, or Tyche Soteira, Tyche savioress. Apuleius in his Metamorphoses identifies the "Fortune who can see" with the savior goddess, Isis, who overcomes the effects of blind Fortune.9

The designation, Savior (Greek: soter), signified a deliverer, preserver, protector, or healer, and was applied both to mortals and immortals, male and female. Saviors in the Greek and Hellenistic world included not only deities like Zeus, Jesus, Serapis, Asclepius, Isis, and Tyche, but also famous men like Plato, Epicurus, Alexander, Ptolemy of Egypt, and the Roman emperors. "Savior," then, designated extraordinary personalities, divine or human, who were active in world affairs, that is, who were considered to have changed or transformed a situation for the better, whether militarily, politically, intellectually, or spiritually.

In the Hellenistic world generally, the individual overcame the effects of ill-fortune through initiation into the Mysteries of a feminine savior deity, commonly imaged as the Mother Goddess. Formerly buffeted by the caprice of Tyche/Fortuna, the initiate now was safe in the protective embrace of the Queenly Mother of Heaven.

The Earth Mother of archaic mythology had become elevated in the Ptolemaic cosmology of the Hellenistic world to the governing luminous position of the night sky, the lunar Queen of Heaven. With this transition of the locus of the goddess from the elemental chthonic aspect of the archaic world to the lunar celestial aspect in the Ptolemaic, the ambiguous Great Mother Goddess became manifest as the twin Good and Terrible Mothers. Hellenistic man experienced, with the arbitrariness of the ruling Feminine, not only the grace of her epiphanies but despair resulting from her absence, the dark side of the feminine withholding herself. Although the patriarchal nature of Western mythology has virtually obliterated the Terrible Mother figure so important, for example in India, she survived into the Hellenistic world. In fact, the dynamics of Hellenistic religiosity is, in part, the dynamics of her obliteration.

Despite the widespread success of the Mysteries in dealing with Tyche/Fortuna, the rule even of good Fortune resulted in the feminine pattern becoming by late antiquity almost exclusively understood as manifest in the unpersonified but wholly negative rule of Heimarmene (Greek: Destiny).10 Heimarmene was the necessary conclusion to the astrological and philosophical emphases on the providential rule of Tyche. If, indeed, in the parallel between the macrocosm and the microcosm, the celestial powers causally ordered terrestrial activity, then this order was bought at the price of an oppressive determinism. Heimarmene represented this oppression, imaged in the embracing spheres of the planetary powers. The embrace of these powers no longer was understood as the nurturing locus of order, but as an imprisoning grasp of death. The symbolically feminine structure of the totality of the cosmos itself was now understood as defective.

With this exclusively negative revaluation of the feminine and of the effects of her cosmic rule, religiosity in late antiquity began to look towards a masculine hypercosmic locus as the origin of life. In other words, the oppressive feminine rule of Heimarmene had become understood as a bondage from which the redemptive goal was escape, escape from the rule of the feminine altogether as well as from the cosmos, because the two were identified. As expressed in one of the Nag Hammadi gnostic texts:

> Flee from the madness and the bondage of femininity, and choose for yourselves the salvation of masculinity. You have come not [to suffer], but to escape your bondage.
>
> --Zostrianos 131, 5-11. 11

The symbolism of redemption in late antiquity, then, perforce took on the symbolism of transcendent masculinity and of anticosmic otherworldliness.

The mythic pattern which arose in response to this anticosmism rejected the transformatory pattern of the feminine oriented saviour cults to establish masculine patterns of transcendence. Contrary to the soter who was active within world affairs, the redeemer rescued or delivered man from the terrestrial condition to which he was bound. These redeemers were always masculine and unlike the title of savior, the title of redeemer is used exclusively of male deities.

Redeemer, (Greek: lutrotes), is used, for example, of Moses in the New Testament who redeemed his followers from the land of Egypt to lead them into the promised land (Acts 7:35). That is to say, lutrosis carries a spatial connotation of transference from one place to another. The masculine redeemers charted, in their descent into this world and in their revelatory reascent, the "Way" back through the celestial spheres for the faithful to follow in their own transcendence of the cosmic Heimarmene. This transition from the earlier pattern of the Mysteries is attested by Clement in the <u>Excerpta</u> <u>ex</u> <u>Theodoto</u>:

> Therefore a strange new star arose doing away with the old astral decree, shining with a new unearthly light, which revolved on a new path of salvation, as the Lord himself, men's guide, who came down to earth to transfer from Heimarmene to his providence those who believed in Christ.

> --Exc. Theod. 74f. 12

With Gnosticism, chaos would no longer be transformed into order within the circumference of a bounded uterine cosmos. Rather a descending-ascending masculine redeemer would deliver man from the feminine grasp of <u>Heimarmene</u>, the enveloping cosmos itself, to transcend the cosmic limitation of the fallen feminine and to participate in the hypercosmic sacrality of the spiritual Father. The revelation of man's prefallen transcendent origin and the invitation by the masculine to return from the illusion of the fallen cosmic condition, dramatically enacted in the revelatory decensus-ascensus pattern, is the essence of Gnosticism.13

This same pattern of masculine transcendence is found in the symbolism of the Mysteries of Mithras. According to the myth, Mithras was miraculously born from generative rock. The Mithraeum, an actual or simulated cave, symbolized not only this petrine origin, but at the same time, it was a replica of the cosmos. To cite the report of Porphyry:

> Because of matter, then, the Cosmos is misty and dim; but because of the power of form for connecting and ordering (which gives Cosmos its name) it is beautiful and pleasing. For this reason, then, it may be properly described as a cave that is pleasant when one first comes upon it because it participates in form, but obscure when one examines its foundations and penetrates with the mind to the depths of it--so that its exterior surface is pleasing and its interior and depths are dark. Similarly, the Persians call the place a cave where they introduce an initiate to the mysteries, revealing to him the path by which souls descend and go back again. For

Eubulus tells us that Zoraster was the first to dedicate a natural cave in honor of Mithras, the creator and father of all. . . . This cave bore for him the image of the Cosmos which Mithras had created.

- - - - -

Not only, however, as we have said, did the ancients make the cave a symbol of the Cosmos i.e. of generated and sensible nature; they also used it as a symbol of all invisible powers, because caves are dark and the essence of these powers is indistinct.

--de antro nympharum 6-7.#14

The initiates' entrance into and exit from the Mithraic cave ritually paralleled the birth of Mithras from the rock and symbolized their rebirth out of the cosmic womb and their mastery over the symbolic feminine. Even as Mithras in his birth ascended from the darkness of the chthonic rock, the cavern of this cosmos, to assume his place as the heroic Sol Invictus, so the initiate exited from the darkness of the chthonic Mithraeum to participate in the light of his transcendent god.

This motif of soteriological ascent is manifest further in the seven grades of the Mithraic initiation. It is imaged as the ascent of a seven runged ladder, each rung representing both a rank of initiation, and one of the seven oppressive planetary spheres. Through the ritual ascent of initiation, the mystae symbolically transcend the conditions of this world.

Similarly, according to the redemptive Christology of Paul, the Christian was able to transcend an oppressive cosmos:

When we were children, we were slaves to the elemental spirits of the universe. But when the time had fully come, God sent forth his Son . . . to redeem those who were under the law.
--Gal. 4:3-5

Formerly, when you did not know God, you were in bondage to beings that by nature

are no gods; but now that you have come to
know God, or rather to be known by God, how
can you turn back again to the weak and
beggarly elemental spirits who slaves you
want to be once more?
                                    --Gal. 4:8f.15

Thus in the Gnostic challenge to Heimarmene, and in
the Mithraic and Pauline challenge to this world,
there emerged a patriarchal challenge to the systemic
dominance of the feminine in the Greco-Roman world.

A Jungian approach to collective situations and
to historical problems such as that presented by
Hellenistic religions suggests structures and
relationships constituative of a systemic totality
which is inaccesible to, or has been only hinted at by
traditional historical scholarship. Thus, Jung's
phenomenology of the feminine suggests an
understanding of an integral and successive
relationship between Tyche/Fortuna and Heimarmene,
whereby Heimarmene represents the rise to historical
dominance of the maleficent side of the differentiated
feminine, Tyche/Fortuna. Further, this phenomenology
suggests an integral relationship between the feminine
rule of this world by a negative Heimarmene and the
general acceptance at the beginning of our era of its
alternative, the masculine rule of a transcendent
Father God. These integral relationships suggest in
turn that religion in the Hellenistic period belonged
to a total system of integrated structures which
allowed for just those religious syncretisms which
occurred and no other, and which organized their
historical particularity. Finally, if the validity
and universality of Jung's psychological model are
accepted, the well-known parallels between cosmology
and mythology might well be extended to anthropology,
thus allowing further insights into the nature of
Hellenistic religious experience.

1. For example, Mircea Eliade, _The Forge and the Crucible_, trans. Stephen Corrin (1956, rpt. New York and Evanston: Harper and Row, 1971), pp. 195ff., and especially 221ff., and _No Souvenirs_, trans. Fred H. Johnson, Jr. (New York, Hagerstown, San Francisco, London: 1977), especially p. xiii; also R. C. Zaehner, _Mysticism_: _Sacred and Profane_ (1957, rpt. London, Oxford, New York: Oxford University Press, 1967), _passim_, but especially p. xv; Gilles Quispel, _Gnosis als Weltreligion_ (Zurich: Origo Verlag, 1972), and _Gnostic Studies_, 2 vols. (Istanbul: Netherlands Institute of History and Archaeology, 1974-1975); Walter L. Brenneman, Jr., _Spirals_: _A Study in Symbol, Myth and Ritual_ (University Press of America, 1977).

2. Although Sigmund Freud generally is included with Karl Marx, Emile Durkheim, and Ferdinand de Saussure as among the forerunners of modern structuralism (see e.g., Richard and Fernande DeGeorge, eds., _The Structuralists_: _From Marx to Levi-Strauss_ (Garden City, New York: Anchor Books, 1972), pp. xvi-xvii; Jonathan Culler, _Ferdinand de Saussure_ (1976, rpt. New York: Penguin Books, 1980), pp. 73-78), his influence is traced through the French intellectual tradition upon the thought, primarily, of Jacques Lacan. The relationship of Jung's archetypal theory to the various structuralist positions has not been examined.

3. C. G. Jung, _Memories, Dreams, Reflections_, recorded and ed. Aniela Jaffe, trans. Richard and Clara Winston (New York: Vintage Books, 1961), p. 84.

4. E.g., F. C. Grant, _Hellenistic Religions_, The Library of Liberal Arts (Indianapolis and New York: The Bobbs-Merrill Company, 1953), p. xiii.

5. See, e.g., with respect to matter and the alchemical work, C. G. Jung, _Psychology and_

Alchemy, trans. R. F. C. Hull, CW 12, 2nd edition
(Princeton: Princeton University Press, 1952),
pp. 228, 278f., 299f.

6. Ptolemy, Tetabiblos I, 1-6, trans. F. E. Robbins.
Loeb Classical Library (Cambridge: Harvard
University Press, 1940).

7. C. G. Jung, The Archetypes and the Collective
Unconscious, trans. R. F. C. Hull, CW 9, i, 2nd
edition (Princeton: Princeton University Press,
1968), p. 81; see also the discussion by Erich
Neumann, The Great Mother, trans. Ralph Manheim,
2nd edition (Princeton: Princeton University
Press, 1963), pp. 230-232.

8. Natural History, Vol. 1, trans. H. Rackham, Loeb
Classical Library (Cambridge, Massachusetts:
Harvard University Press, 1944).

9. Metamorphoses, xi, 15, trans. W. Adlington, rev.
S. Gaselee, Loeb Classical Library (Cambridge,
Massachusetts: Harvard University Press, 1965).

10. Both Neumann in his comprehensive analysis of the
Great Mother archetype and Jung treat the figures
of Tyche/Fortuna and of Heimarmene only in
passing.

11. Trans. John H. Sieber, in The Nag Hammadi
Library, James M. Robinson, gen. ed. (New York,
Hagerstown, San Francisco, London: Harper and
Row, 1977), p. 393.

12. Trans. Robert Pierce Casey (London:
Christophers, 1934).

13. Ugo Bianchi, ed., The Origins of Gnosticism
(Leiden: E. J. Brill, 1967), pp. xxvif.

14. Porphyry, The Cave of the Nymphs in the Odyssey,
text and trans. by Seminar Classics 609, Arethusa
Monographs No. 1 (Department of Classics, State
University of New York at Buffalo, 1969).

15. See H. D. Betz, Galatians (Philadelphia:
Fortress Press, 1979), p. 204.

SECTION III

C. G. JUNG, JAMES HILLMAN, AND

THE STUDY OF RELIGION

143

CHAPTER 9

DIFFERENCES BETWEEN JUNG AND HILLMAN:

IMPLICATIONS FOR A PSYCHOLOGY OF RELIGION

James A. Hall, M.D.

Jung's analytical psychology is one of the most
promising directions of movement at the interface of
depth psychology and religion.1   Jung regards the
"deeper" unconscious as containing the "image of God,"
which can be seen in some archetypal images, dreams,
and imaginal experiences.   Jung's concern with
science, particularly the relation of psyche and
matter, opens a promising horizon for natural
theology: is there empirical evidence of a natural
religious function in the human psyche?   It is
therefore important to differentiate the essential
structure of Jung's thought from secondary
elaborations in the Jungian literature.   One of the
most confusing areas of the secondary Jungian
literature is "archetypal psychology," a movement
founded primarily upon the writings of James Hillman,
a Jungian analyst and former director of studies at
the C. G. Jung Institute, Zurich, and editor of
Spring, a publication originally sponsored by the
Analytical Psychology Club of New York but now
entirely under the editorial direction of Hillman.
Hillman has accused the Jungian clinical tradition of
reification of concepts in a "monotheistic" direction.
I believe Hillman to be mistaken.   In any case, it is
necessary to disentangle Jung's position from
Hillman's presentation of it before we can thoroughly
evaluate the exciting implications of Jung's thought
for the psychology of religion.2   This paper,
therefore, will discuss similarities and differences
between the classical Jungian tradition and the

movement that Hillman has christened "archetypal psychology."

Hillman's two outstanding contributions to Jungian thought have been his elaboration of selected archetypal images, particularly from Greek mythology, and his tireless vigilance against reification of concepts. Hillman neglects, however, certain basic Jungian areas such as the concept of Self; his elaboration of archetypal themes in myth and literature (e.g., the puer and senex) is several levels removed from the usual concern of clinical Jungian analysis. It is possible that Hillman misunderstands Jung in several vital areas: the nature of the ego, the structure of the Self, the relationship of the ego-Self "axis," and the functional nature of such structural concepts as anima and animus, which clinically can be seen to have a relatively fixed structure, but not a fixed content.

The present review cannot hope to be exhaustive of the writings of either Jung or Hillman, nor does it closely examine the still-developing nature of Hillman's position (there are many excerpts in Spring from "works in progress"). It may be useful, however, to mark certain signposts within Hillman's writings. Insearch, a small book originally published in 1967 and reissued in 1979, shows Hillman's thought at that time (1967) to be entirely consistent with the main currents of Jungian tradition: the terms shadow and anima are used in a traditional sense; there is firm appreciation of the need for a tension of opposites to be held in consciousness; the "demonic" can be located in either the collective unconscious or in the outer world of collective consciousness; and Hillman speaks of the self (which he styles without a capital initial letter) in a classical sense:

> Wanting forgiveness to come and waiting for it may be all the ego can do; the rest must come, if it does, from the self.3

Only three years later, however, in "Why 'Archetypal' Psychology?," Hillman produces a manifesto in introducing the new subtitle "a journal of archetypal psychology" to Spring.4 The "eponym Jungian" was rejected for reasons that included: ". . . Jungian derives from a family name and belongs to an actual family rather than to a following."5 The term complex psychology, also used by Jung for his psychology, was considered by Hillman to refer too much to the possibly empirical basis of Jung's observations:

> As the name indicates, complex psychology builds upon the complex for its theory. This basis is empirical because it takes up the complex mainly through the association experiment, where measurements play the major role. . . . Nevertheless, the designation has one great disadvantage: it evokes Jung's first idea of the complex as a <u>disturbance</u> of consciousness.6

The term that Jung himself preferred was <u>analytical</u> <u>psychology</u>, but Hillman discards this name with the comment that at the time Jung used it he had not yet worked out his concept of the archetype, and more important to Hillman:

> Placing archetypal prior to analytical gives the psyche a chance to move out of the consulting room. It gives an archetypal perspective to the consulting room itself. After all, analysis too is an enactment of an archetypal fantasy.7

Hillman continues to prefer "archetypal psychology" to the term <u>analytical psychology</u>, stating that ". . . we do not have to take the archetypes as primarily <u>psychic</u> structures; the psyche is only one place where they manifest."8 Hillman neglects to point out that Jung himself clearly stated that the archetypes may be <u>psychoid</u>, that is, they may be a structure behind both consciousness <u>and</u> the physical world.9 It is in this essay that Hillman also introduces "what might be called a polytheistic psychology" and takes a stand against traditional psychoanalysis and psychotherapy, stating that:

> The problems of the psyche were never solved in classical times nor by archaic peoples through personal relationships and 'humanizing', but through the reverse: connecting them to impersonal dominants.10

How far Hillman has veered away from his position in <u>Insearch</u> is evident in his statement that:

> The plurality of archetypal forms reflects that pagan level of things and what might be

called polytheistic psychology. It provides for many varieties of consciousness, styles of existence, and ways of soul making, thereby freeing individuation from stereotypes of an ego on the road to a Self [his capital]. By reflecting this plurality and freedom of styles within the structures of myth, the archtypal perspective of experience may be furthered. In this spirit Spring hopes to proceed.11

Hillman thus dismisses the term Jungian psychology as too personal, complex psychology as too objective and caught in "the empirical fantasy," and the most traditional term analytical psychology as too clinical. Although the new term "archetypal psychology" is presented as an extension of Jung's more mature interests, it is clear that Hillman intends to focus on literary sources, largely omitting from consideration two of Jung's most vital and enduring interests: the clinical care of suffering persons and the value of scientific investigation.

In 1971 Hillman published in Spring an essay titled "Psychology: Monotheistic or Polytheistic."12 This marks the clear turning point at which Hillman is no longer speaking of ego and Self as he did in Insearch. He either discards, or perhaps misunderstands Jung's meaning of Self, which Jung called "the archetype which it is most important for modern man to understand."13 For example, Hillman asserts that in Aion Jung "implies that as anima/animus is a pre-stage of self, so is polytheism a pre-stage of monotheism."14 Hillman then contrasts a psychology based on Self with one based on "the plurality of the archetypes" and re-asserts a definitional statement of his own "archetypal psychology": "Archetypal psychology begins with Jung's notion of the complexes whose archetypal cores are bases for all psychic life whatsoever."

My own reading of Jung does not suggest that he at any point considers anima/animus as a pre-stage of Self, since that would be to present as a dynamic movement in time what is a structural distinction only. Jung consistently presents the Self as embodying the action of all archetypes. Far from presenting the Self as a monolithic unitary force, as Hillman implies, Jung actually discusses the structure of the Self in the final chapter of Aion.15 There

147

Jung pictures the relativity of such images as the Old Wise Man, which Hillman has equated with the Self.16 Another frequent image of the Self, the structure of crystals, can be seen in Jung's diagram as implicit in the various personified roles (such as Moses, the Ethopian woman, the lapis, etc.).17 Hillman attributes to Jung a constricted view that Jung does not hold; Hillman then proceeds to offer a "wider" point of view, which in essence is narrower than Jung's vision of the psyche.

It is also in "Psychology: Monotheistic or Polytheistic" that Hillman adds Christianity to his list of enemies:

> Where once science, and then clinical pragmatics were the enemies of the psyche, today the threat to the psyche's freedom of symbol-formation is nothing else than fading Christianity coming back in the guise of a theology of the Self to claim the soul for its own.18

At this point--1975--I must question whether Hillman is still representative of the main currents of Jungian thought and practice.

Symbol and "Image"

Symbol, a basic Jungian concept, is presented in a non-traditional way by Hillman in a 1977 essay "An Inquiry into Image" published in Spring.19 While presumably perfectly aware of the classical Jungian distinction between symbol and sign, Hillman's dialectical essay ignores this meaning and instead substitutes the term "image" for what in Jungian usage would be symbol. Hillman speaks of symbol as Jungians would speak of sign, using the ostensible justification that "Our practice with symbols no longer accords with our theory of them," making a distinction between ". . . Jung's theory of symbols and the practice of looking them up.20 Hillman substitutes the term "imagistically" for the usual Jungian usage of the term symbolically:

> If we focus on the whenever and wherever of an image, its generality and conventionality, we are looking at it symbolically. If, on the other hand, we examine the how of a symbol, its

148

> particularity and peculiarness, then we are
> looking at it imagistically.21

> The (symbols) are abstractions from images.
> (Else we couldn't look them up.)22

> Any image that is taken as a symbol, by
> being stepped up to universal size, is no
> longer an image. The symbolic approach
> contradicts the imagistic, and this mainly
> because the symbolic approach offers
> generality at the cost of precision.23

In each of these statements, if the traditional term
symbol is substituted for "image," the term sign for
"symbol," and the usual term symbolic for "imagistic,"
then Hillman is speaking conventional Jungian maxims.
It is of course perfectly acceptable for Hillman (or
anyone) to introduce a new usage of language, but to
do so without discussion of usual meanings, and on the
basis of his (incorrect, in my opinion) judgement of
current Jungian practice, introduces unnecessary and
unwarranted confusion, particularly for a reader who
is unacquainted with the corpus of Jungian literature
and knows of Jung and Jungian practice only through
the eyes of Hillman.

Structural Concepts: Ego, Anima/Animus, Shadow and Self

Because Hillman uses traditional Jungian terms in
non-traditional ways, redefining (as with symbol), and
altering emphasis, it is necessary briefly to compare
certain basic structural terms of analytical
psychology, contrasting their meaning with the usage
of Hillman.

Ego

Hillman generally speaks negatively of ego,
seeming to equate it with excessive order, which he
attributes to "the negative senex," even stating that
"the high God of our culture is a senex god."24 In
"The 'Negative' Senex and a Renaissance Solution"
Hillman draws tighter the connection of ego, as he
sees it, with the archetypal structure called
"senex."25

> We have let the basic dualism of the
> structure force us into taking a stand, the

familiar ego stance of positive or negative position. It is this division itself, and not what we judge to be positive or negative, that puts us into senex consciousness. All such judgements about an archetype are from the ego . . . In making this "negative" judgement it is guided by the senex.26

The final triumph of the compulsion to order is ego formation.27

Earlier, Hillman spoke disparagingly of ego in another paper related to the senex, "On Senex Consciousness":

The ego is a superstition born of solitude, a magical way of entering the world of full human being. Call it an enacted omnipotence fantasy.28

Whenever we make order we ask the senex to enter.29

In contrast, Jung presents the concept of ego as "a highly complex affair full of unfathomable obscurities," even stating that "one could even define it as a relatively constant personification of the unconscious itself."30 Jung's view of the ego, unlike Hillman's, places the excessive concreteness not in the action of the ego, but in the failure of the ego to experience the unconscious. Jung states:

The unconscious demands your interest for its own sake and wants to be accepted for what it is. Once the existence of this opposite is accepted, the ego can and should come to terms with its demands. Unless the content given you by the unconscious is acknowledged, its compensatory effect is not only nullified but actually changes into its opposite, as it then tries to realize itself literally and concretely.31

For Jung, then, excessive concreteness (which both Jung and Hillman oppose) is produced by the unconscious in reaction to a failure of the ego to be open to compensatory movements in the unconscious. What Hillman seems to mean by concreteness is the ego attitude that Jung, too, opposes, but Hillman locates the concreteness within an ego-senex structure, not as

150

a literalized compensation to it, as does Jung.

Anima/Animus

Hillman's re-working of _anima_ appears in two successive essays in Spring, 197332 and 1974,33 and throws light not only upon _anima_ in his system, but continues his constriction of _ego_ to the hero myth, which he then rejects. In these essays there is little mention of Jung's central concept of the _Self_.

Hillman's polemic against the ego-Self model complicates his distributive exposition of the anima concept. It is difficult to untangle the connections he makes, and almost impossible without clinical experience of the concept _anima_ in practical dream-interpretation and actual conflict, particularly among married partners. Hillman's main points are:

1. Jung writes from within "a fantasy of opposites."

2. When anima is equated with "soul," the sexual assignment of anima (men supposedly have it and women do not) is incorrect.

3. Anima is "soul" and _animus_ (the corresponding masculine figure in the unconscious of a woman) is "spirit."

4. But both men and women have both soul and spirit, so there must be projection _within_ the unconscious, each anima figure having an animus correlated with it; Hillman can conclude that both men and women have anima _and_ animus.

5. To correct the supposed imbalance, Hillman makes a theoretical caveat, assigning to anima the _basis_ of consciousness and turning the ego into animus:

I suspect that the archetype behind the ego of Western culture as it has issued into ego psychology would reveal itself as the animus, that, in fact, ego is an animus idea. An animus that loses its soul (anima) connection, that posts itself as independent

151

of the syzygy, is ego. The 'weak ego' would be the one affected by the syzygy with anima, and 'strengthening the ego' would mean strengthening the animus. Ego may be heroic in <u>content</u>, but as a psychic <u>function</u> it derives from animus, enacting particular projections of anima. As a function of this syzygy, ego cannot have a valid identity of its own.34

6. Continuing his attack upon the ego (which he sees only as "heroic") Hillman seeks to re-introduce the sex-assignment of anima and animus as inevitable:

The archetypal perspective of the syzygy will always perceive events in compensatory paring.35

Nonetheless, essential to thinking in syzygies is thinking in genders.36

Indeed, it seems that much of what we have been calling ego is the animus-half of the syzygy.37

In his own stance toward the anima, Jung recommends objectification of the anima as a first step toward investigating what is behind anima tendencies.38 Jung attributes the "personality" of anima to the function of the anima being "autonomous and undeveloped."39 It is not that the anima or animus is to be depotentiated in favor of the ego, but "by making them conscious we convert them into bridges to the unconscious." Jung treats the anima with the same regard as if "she" were another person, but does not recommend relativizing the ego in favor of the anima (or any other archetypal content):

So long as the affect is speaking, criticism must be withheld. But once it has presented its case, we should begin criticizing as conscientiously as though a real person closely connected with us were our interlocutor. Nor should the matter rest there, but statement and answer must follow one another until a satisfactory end to the discussion is reached. Whether the result is satisfactory or not only subjective feeling can decide. . . . Scrupulous

honesty with oneself and no rash
anticipation of what the other side might
conceivably say are the indispensable
conditions of this technique. . .40

In the next paragraph, Jung adds:

And here I would expressly point out that I
am not recommending the above technique as
either necessary or even useful to any
person not driven to it by necessity.

Jung, unlike Hillman, presents a model of
intentional and careful interaction with the anima,
not to pull anima or animus into consciousness (which
is, in any case, not possible) but in order to
assimilate what can be assimilated, opening the door
wider to further and deeper contact between
consciousness and the unconscious. This description
of conversation with the anima, which approximates
active imagination, places the ego in the position
that Jung recommends: as the responsible
representative in consciousness of the unconscious,
particularly the ordering property of the Self.41 It
is clear that the ego is not taking a "monotheistic"
heroic stance, but treating the anima as an equal.
Far from Hillman's formula of ego=animus, Jung states:

Although the two figures (anima and animus)
are always tempting the ego to identify
itself with them, a real understanding even
on the personal level is possible only if
the identification is refused.
Nonidentification demands considerable moral
effort. Moreover it is only legitimate when
not used as a pretext to avoid the necessary
degree of personal understanding.42

Self

Self is seldom mentioned by Hillman, but is a
central concept in Jung's thought. Jung speaks of the
Self in several ways, including (a) the totality of
the psyche, (b) the archetypal core of the ego, and
(c) as the archetypal image of the ordered wholeness
of the psyche, often presenting in mandala symbolism.
Jung states:

As an empirical concept, the self designates
the whole range of psychic phenomena in man.

It expresses the unity of the personality as a whole.43

I have defined the self as the totality of the conscious and the unconscious psyche, and the ego as the central reference-point of consciousness. It is an essential part of the self, and can be used pars pro toto when the significance of consciousness is borne in mind. But when we want to lay emphasis on the psychic totality it is better to use the term "self." There is no question of a contradictory definition, but merely of a difference of standpoint.44

The ego is the only content of the self that we do know. The individuated ego senses itself as the object of an unknown and supraordinate subject.45

This last insight, the individuating ego sensing that it is part of a larger subjectivity, is echoed by Jung in his autobiography, citing two dreams of his own.46 It is this sense of being subordinate to a greater personality that is at the same time the deeper part of oneself that I believe Hillman is trying over and over to emphasize by "relativizing" the ego in favor of various archetypal contents. Jung points to the same phenomenology, however, in a way that does not diminish or discard ego, but relativizes it in the service of Self, the totality of the psyche, both conscious and unconscious. Thus Jung's view is a more thoroughly relational, interactive model than the one Hillman seeks to place in its stead. Hillman seems to vision only a static ego that must be relativized in favor of a large and indeterminate number of archetypal forms; Jung suggests a stable ego that is yet in relation to a myriad of archetypal forms that are coordinated in the totality of the Self.

Hillman repeatedly presents ego as based upon the hero archetype. This static view pervades Hillman's critique of Jung, in spite of it appearing on the surface to favor relativization over fixity. What is missing is Jung's appreciation of the ego as the container that is necessary for the unification of opposites as well as a lack of clinical understanding of what "unification of opposites" actually means. The "unification of opposites" does not mean a sacrifice of one for the other, nor does it connote the mean or median between the opposite poles; rather, it means exactly what Jung says of the Self: it is a complexio oppositorum in which both opposites participate, as in the t'ai chi tu image of yang/yin in Taoism.47 This subtlety of Jung's thought is evident throughout his Collected Works, but notably in the concluding chapter of Aion, "The Structure and Dynamics of the Self." There the Self is shown as having schematic inner structure in which, paradoxically, the "highest" and the "lowest" points of development are joined. This structure of the Self contains both masculine and feminine identities, it is not the saturnian senex of Hillman's exposition. Elsewhere Jung speaks to the subtle relationship of the ego (the "I") and the Self, imaged as Christ:

> It [individuation] is not an "imitation of Christ" but its exact opposite: an assimilation of the Christ-image to his own self, which is the "true man."48

In a footnote to this statement, Jung adds as amplification that the true man "is not to be confused with the ego."

In a passage reminiscent of St. Paul struggling to communicate what was perhaps the same mysterious unity/separateness of the ego/Self, Jung describes the relationship of the alchemical adept to the work:

> The Passion happens to the adept, not in its classical form--otherwise he would be consciously performing spiritual exercises--but in the form expressed by the alchemical myth. It is the arcane substance that suffers those physical and moral tortures; it is the king who dies or is killed, is dead and buried and on the third day rises again. And it is not the adept who suffers all this, rather it suffers in him, it is tortured, it passes through death and rises again. All this happens not to the alchemist himself but to the "true man," who he feels is near him and in him and at the same time in the retort.49

For Jung, but not for Hillman, the Self is a horizon of the ego, drawing it onward into individuation. This horizon, if sufficiently extended, becomes the inner image of God. Jung belongs within the present discussions of natural theology by such scientists as Sir John Eccles.50

Science

Jung viewed himself as clearly within the scientific tradition, an important factor in the contributions of Jungian thought to questions, such as those of natural theology or process theology, that arise at the interface of science and religion. His autobiographical work Memories, Dreams, Reflections was, by his express decision, excluded from his Collected Works. As his secretary and collaborator Aneilia Jaffe stated, it was only in the autobiography that Jung permitted himself to speak of "God"; elsewhere he is careful to speak within more scientific bounds of "the image of God in the psyche."51

Jung's training was within the medical and scientific world, and before choosing medicine he had ambition to be an Egyptologist.52 There are other evidences of Jung's intent to remain within the scientific tradition, even while exploring the religious depths of the psyche in mythology, religion, and within alchemy, primordial amalgam of Western religion and science. Jung's initial work with the word-association experiment placed him clearly within the empirical scientific tradition, although one can note even there his perception of subtle meanings, such as work with the physiological correlates of emotional states, the similarity of word-association patterns within families, and use of measurements to assess unreported guilty feelings.

Jung's typology has been the basis for many empirical studies and a number of typological tests: Gray-Wheelwright, Meyer-Briggs, and Singer-Loomis. Although Jung wrote before the rise of laboratory sleep and dream research, his study of dreams moved in a direction that bridges readily toward empirical questions, although as yet few researchers have designed dream experiments on Jungian hypothesis.53

Synchronicity

Jung's most profound concern with the empirical nature of reality appears in his concept of synchronicity, which "points to a profound harmony between all forms of existence."54 In a letter to Carleton Smith, Jung praised the work of J. B. Rhine, the father of modern parapsychology, for his work on the nature of the psyche.55 In a letter to Rhine himself Jung wrote:

> I often mention your work to people over here and I think it is of the greatest importance for the understanding of certain peculiar phenomena of the unconscious. In our practical work we come across peculiar telepathic influences which throw a most significant light on the relativity of space and time in our unconscious psyche. I quite agree with you that once we are in possession of all facts science will look very peculiar indeed. It will mean nothing less than an entirely new understanding of man and world.56

In 1977, Rhine himself spoke of "The Parapsychology of Religion: A New Branch of Inquiry," echoing Jung's concern that parapsychology may show empirically connections between the psyche and the world:

> First is the question of whether a person can exercise some volitional control over his situation. Is he in any meaningful sense (and in even the slightest verifiable degree) a free moral agent--free that is, of the substituent deterministic forces operating in and through his organism? Second is the problem of man's post-mortem destiny, whether or not death is the end of the personality as an individual agent. Third is the question of the kind of universe it is in which we live. Is it in any verifiable way a personal universe with a type of intelligently purposive agency within it to which man can with rational confidence turn for helpful communicatin in the midst of the trying emergencies of life? . . . For one thing, these are obviously much more than problems of parapsychology alone. But it does now seem safe to say with some confidence that this branch [of science] can continue to make advances into problem areas of religion where the footprints of no other science have ever been left.57

Hillman's interest in parapsychology, a major evidence of Jung's scientific commitment, is limited to one essay, in which he omits reference to Jung's concern with an empirical demonstration of the phenomena of the unus mundus. Hillman linked parapsychology to "an activity of the spirit" that he stated was "irreducible to any other component."58 In contrast to the hopefulness of Jung and Rhine, Hillman came to an essentially nihilistic and anti-empirical conclusion:

> Perhaps as someone here remarked, quoting William James, the Creator does not want us to understand. Perhaps parapsychology refers not to what we do not yet know, but what we may never know, because it is unknowable.59

Hillman's attitude toward parapsychology contrasts with Jung's clearly stated position:

> In cases where neither our sense organs nor their artificial aids can attest the presence of a real object, the difficulties mount enormously, so that one feels tempted to assert that there is simply no real object present. I have never drawn this overhasty conclusion for I have never been inclined to think that our senses were capable of perceiving all forms of being.60

Jung and Hillman: Contrasts

I believe that I understand Hillman's primary purpose of "seeing through" the basic assumptions behind conscious positions, which of course is a statement of the basic psychotherapeutic technique in the treatment of neurosis, a statement with which I (and all depth psychologists) must agree. But Hillman over-reaches his purpose in suggesting that he is rescuing Jung from the "Jungians" when in fact he is reifying the ego and collective consciousness and then (having artificially constructed the problem) suggesting that the proper solution is deliteralizing, "seeing through," dissolving the sense of the real and taking the "soul" into the "underworld" of multiple gods and goddesses. Such an "underworld" is protection only from a reification of the everyday, consensual world.

Hillman's massive detour is not necessary, for Jung himself offers a more subtle analysis of the problem. Jung sees all the world as primordially unus mundus, for which synchronicity is both personal and scientific evidence. Jung affirms that the world is and that one is connected to the image of God, through whatever convolutions of the psyche that connexion may be seen. The Christian world for Jung is anything but a sterile "monotheistic" tyranny; it is a still-unfolding archetypal movement, disclosing as-yet-not-anticipated mysteries. In the Christian world, as seen by Jung, the proclamation of the assumption of Mary is not a minor variant within the mind of the Pope, but indicates an organic growth of the psyche itself, of its image of God, toward an understanding of the unus mundus and the archetypal image of the anthropos. Science and the consulting room are an integral part of this archetypal unfolding, not the by-paths away from "soul" that Hillman states.

In spite of his intentions, Hillman is not rescuing Jung, he is confining, molding, constricting Jung into a supposed corrective to a literalized collective consciousness. Jung himself is broader and deeper than Hillman. Jung offers the modern world the most promising window yet through which to see that life is more than personal, more than mere individuality--that it is individuation, part of the life process and history of the planet, of the universe, of God.

Summary

Jungian psychology has become increasingly important in conceptualizing a psychology of religion that appreciates the unconscious depths of the human personality. Because many persons approach Jung's thought through the writings of Hillman's "archetypal psychology," it is important to note significantly different emphases in Jung and Hillman. Although based on Jungian thought, Hillman's "archetypal psychology" stresses the phenomenological form of Jung's writings at the expense of Jung's lifelong concern to speak scientifically while remaining true to his clinical insights about the individual psyche. Jung showed great respect for the ego, for a personal standpoint in relation to the unconscious, while "archetypal psychology" places little stress on

159

ego-psychology or the related clinical concerns of healing. The Jungian concept of the Self, the central archetype of order, is the least empirical of Jung's structural terms but the one most related to religious experience. While largely ignoring the Self, "archetypal psychology" stresses a multiplicity of god-images presented as personified archetypes without the co-ordinating center of the Self.

Analytical psychology (Jung's own term) offers a wider field for understanding psychology of religion than does the constricted form of Jung's thought that Hillman has presented as "archetypal psychology." A clear understanding of Jung is essential to bring his thought to bear upon current questions of natural theology as raised by Rhine, Polanyi, Eccles, and others.

NOTES

1. James Hall, "Psychiatry and Religion: A Review and a Projection of Future Needs," <u>Anglican Theological Review</u>, LXIII (4), October 1981, pp. 422-435.

2. <u>Ibid</u>.

3. James Hillman, <u>Insearch</u> (Dallas: Spring Publications, 1979), p. 73.

4. James Hillman, "Why 'Archetypal' Psychology?," <u>Spring</u> 1970, pp. 212-219.

5. <u>Ibid</u>., p. 212.

6. <u>Ibid</u>., p. 213.

7. <u>Ibid</u>., p. 216.

8. <u>Ibid</u>.

9. C. G. Jung, <u>The Structure and Dynamics of the Psyche</u>, <u>Collected Works</u>, Vol. 8, translated by R. F. C. Hull (Princeton: Princeton University Press, 1960), pp. 215f.

10. Hillman, "Why 'Archetypal' Psychology?," p. 218.

11. <u>Ibid</u>., pp. 218-219.

12. James Hillman, "Psychology: Monotheistic or Polytheistic," <u>Spring</u> 1971, pp. 193-208.

13. C. G. Jung, <u>Aion</u>, <u>Collected Works</u>, Vol. 9, II, translated by R. F. C. Hull (Princeton: Princeton University Press, 1968), p. 266.

14. James Hillman, <u>Re-Visioning Psychology</u> (New York: Harpers, 1975), p. 193.

15. Jung, <u>Aion</u>, p. 222-65.

16. Hillman, "Psychology: Monotheistic or Polytheistic," p. 196.

17. Jung, _Aion_, p. 227-32.

18. Hillman, "Psychology: Monotheistic or Polytheistic," p. 204.

19. James Hillman, "An Inquiry into Image," _Spring_ 1977, pp. 62-88.

20. _Ibid._, pp. 68 and 67.

21. _Ibid._, p. 64.

22. _Ibid._, p. 65.

23. _Ibid._, p. 66.

24. James Hillman, "On Senex Consciousness," _Spring_ 1970, pp. 146-165.

25. James Hillman, "The 'Negative' Senex and a Renaissance Solution," _Spring_ 1975, pp. 77-109.

26. _Ibid._, p. 89.

27. _Ibid._, p. 90.

28. Hillman, "On Senex Consciousness," p. 162.

29. _Ibid._, p. 150.

30. C. G. Jung, _Mysterium Coniunctionis, Collected Works_, Vol. 14, translated by R. F. C. Hull (Princeton: Princeton University Press, 1970), p. 107.

31. _Ibid._, p. 162.

32. James Hillman, "Anima," _Spring_ 1973, pp. 97-132.

33. James Hillman, "Anima II," _Spring_ 1974, pp. 113-146.

34. _Ibid._, p. 143.

35. _Ibid._, p. 139.

36. _Ibid._, p. 141.

37. _Ibid._, p. 143.

38. C. G. Jung, _Two Essays on Analytical Psychology_, _Collected Works_, Vol. 7, translated by R. F. C. Hull (Princeton: Princeton University Press, 1966), p. 200.

39. _Ibid._, p. 210.

40. _Ibid._, pp. 202f.

41. See C. G. Jung, _Civilization in Transition_, Collected Works, Vol. 10, translated by R. F. C. Hull (Princeton: Princeton University Press, 1970), p. 424 and _Psychology and Alchemy_, _Collected Works_, Vol. 12, translated by R. F. C. Hull (Princeton: Princeton University Press, 1968), p. 25.

42. C. G. Jung, _The Practice of Psychotherapy_, _Collected Works_, Vol. 16, translated by R. F. C. Hull (Princeton: Princeton University Press, 1971), p. 261.

43. _Psychological Types_, p. 460.

44. _Mysterium Coniunctionis_, p. 110.

45. _Two Essys on Analytical Psychology_, p. 240.

46. C. G. Jung, _Memories, Dreams, Reflections_, edited by Aniela Jaffe, translated by Richard and Clara Winston (New York: Random House, 1961), p. 323.

47. _Aion_, p. 225, 267.

48. _Mysterium Coniunctionis_, p. 349.

49. _Ibid_.

50. John C. Eccles, _The Human Psyche_ (New York: Springer International, 1980).

51. In the introduction to Jung's _Memories, Dreams, Reflections_, p. xi.

52. C. G. Jung, _C. G. Jung Speaking: Interviews and Encounters_, edited by Willima McGuire and R. F. C. Hull (Princeton: Princeton University Press, 1977), p. 428.

53. C. G. Jung, *Experimental Researches, Collected Works*, Vol. 2, translated by Leopold Stein with Diana Riviere (Princeton: Princeton University Press, 1972), p. 33-35.

54. *Aion*, p. 261.

55. C. G. Jung, *Letters*, Vol. 2, edited by G. Adler (Princeton: Princeton University Press, 1977), p. 124.

56. *Ibid.*, Vol. 1, p. 321.

57. J. B. Rhine, "The Parapsychology of Religion: A New Branch of Inquiry," *Journal*, Texas Society for Psychical Research and Oklahoma SPR, 1977-1978.

58. James Hillman, "On the Psychology of Parapsychology," in *Loose Ends* (Zurich: Spring Publications, 1975), p. 135.

59. *Ibid.*

60. *Memories, Dreams, Reflections*, p. 351.

Except for published volumes, Hillman's papers appear largely in *Spring*, an annual for which he has editorial responsibility. Originally sponsored by the Analytical Psychology Club of New York, which has since dissociated itself from *Spring*, there have been various publication places: New York, Zurich, Dallas. *Spring* is currently available from the Institute for Humanities and Culture, 2719 Routh Street, Dallas, Texas 75201.

CHAPTER 10

ANIMA IN RELIGIOUS STUDIES

Thomas Moore

Jung was fond of analyzing human experience in the language of opposites, tandems, syzygies, compensations, marriages, conjunctions, unions, and hermaphrodites. His notions of anima and animus, central to his psychology, divide experience into two fundamental qualities, one essentially soul and the other spirit. Secondary literature on Jung's thought tends to discuss anima and animus in terms of gender, yet a quick look at jung's own extensive writing on this theme shows that he was concerned with qualities of experience and reflection. Anima is reflective, relational, imagistic, deep, not sharply defined, moody and atmospheric. Animus, on the other hand, is characterized by thought, judgment, deed, power, and the upper regions of spirit. It is true, Jung identifies these respective modes with gender images. Anima is feminine, and when an ego identifies with a masculine persona, the feminine anima remains unconscious and is projected upon women or imagined in itself as feminine.1

It is fully in accord with Jung's thought, then, to analyze a field of study, such as religious studies, on the paradigm of anima and animus. The field itself is like a patient, given to identifications, compensations, projections, and other forms of unconsciousness. By putting the field on the couch we may be able to spot lacunae and exaggerations that give scholarship a neurotic twist or at least a few symptoms of ill-functioning.

Religious studies follows scholarship in general

as it favors the animus in its style, values, expectations, methodologies, and criteria. The scholar is expected to have control of his material, to proceed with logical, coherent, systematic, rigorous, conceptual or quantitative analysis of data from religions. He should have clear and explicit presuppositions and methodology. His work should fit into current debate and fix itself with regard to the inherited tradition of the field. In religious studies in particular, it often happens that the scholar takes pains to be objective, knowing that the roots of his discipline are tangled in piety, preaching, moralism, and intolerant commitments.

Phenomenology of the animus has been developed further by Jung's revisionist, James Hillman, who emphasizes the notion of "senex." Senex is Latin for "old man," typified in mythology by the Roman God Saturn, the cold, distant, conservative, controlling, depressive figure who is the source of philosophical and religious wisdom. The tandem image for the senex is "puer," "young boy," whose style involves ambition, idealism, flightiness, novelty, experiment, play, and unbounded fantasy. Both styles have their obvious strengths and troublesome tendencies. Both could be seen as sub-images of animus.

Although religious studies appears to have qualities of both puer and senex, with an emphasis on senex, there is little evidence for anima. The masculine element dominates. The critical, authoritative animus is in charge. The softer, fuzzier, less defined, less authoritative contributions of anima are tinged with shadow and felt to be inferior, a threat indeed to good scholarship. There is no dearth of publications and lectures on the feminine as an object of study, but the feminine as a style of scholarship is another matter. Yet, in Jung's therapeutic thought, the marriage, the syzygy, and an androgynous pattern are desirable.

In order to arrive at an idea of what an anima strain in religious studies would be like, we have first to investigate further into Jung's notion of anima. He describes anima as the "inward face," "turned towards the unconscious."2 Anima is a "bridge to the unconscious,"3 a psychopomp, a guide to consciousness in its wanderings. Not ego, but anima leads consciousness. Like Eve from Adam's rib, anima is part of the structure of human being, but at the

166

same time it is apart, more like a companion wedded to consciousness than something under the skin. Anima is not part of the ego-personality, it is something encountered as if different and separate.

For Jung anima is a "function of relationship to the unconscious."4   Typically we use the word "consciousness" to describe an animus style of awareness, and in that context anima is different from consciousness.   But, extending our very notion of consciousness, we might speak of an "anima consciousness," the function of which is not to explain and control but to point to the unknown and give image to it.   Anima reflection remains in the mode of imagination. This function Jung places on a level with what is usually understood as consciousness.   He says of an image of alchemical coniunctio: "The coronation, apotheosis, and marriage signal the equal status of conscious and unconscious."5   Previously he had observed: "This more exalted attitude raises the status of anima from that of temptress to a psychopomp."6   It is not unusual in Jungian psychology to experience anima as a temptation, a seduction away from clear, critical thought toward boundless musings. Scholarship, too, tends to see the seductress in the anima and misses the psychopomp.

Hillman extends these ideas of Jung on anima and underscores the value of anima kinds of reflection:

> Anima explanations point to the unconscious and make us more unconscious. She mystifies, produces sphinx-like riddles, prefers the cryptic and occult where she can remain hidden: she insists upon uncertainty. By leading whatever is known from off its solid footing, she carries every question into deeper waters, which is also a way of soul-making.7

Anima, Hillman goes on, makes us aware of the nature of our unconsciousness. That in itself, of course, is a form of knowledge.

Anima intelligence is surrounded by mist and darkness.   Clarity is not necessarily one of its values.   As Hillman says, "Consciousness is buried in our least aware perspectives."8   To be led into those pockets of unconsciousness is an achievement of anima reflection, where the purpose is to be led and not necessarily to overcome the darkness. To be unaware of the foci of one's unconsciousness is to be blind to the possibility of further reflection and movement.

A further contribution of anima, not ego, says Hillman, is a sense of personality. For the individual, a deep sense of personality does not derive from a strong or colorful ego, but from response to movements felt from within. The more one tries to be a person, the more empty the personality becomes. But as one responds to fate and to the movements of the psyche, a sharper sense of unique identity appears. Interpersonal relationship is created as well by anima. It is common in Jungian circles to describe relationship as anima projection, emphasizing the illusory quality of the fantasy. But to say that anima is involved in relationship is to give soul to the relationship and to acknowledge the intense and expansive eruption of fantasy and feeling that appears in relationship.

While these qualities of anima, furthering personality and relationship, have to do with persons, anima also plays a corresponding role in study. It affords the important sense of relatedness to material. In anima the imagination and feelings are quickened, so that the objects of study have a relationship to the psyche of the scholar and to the psyche of the culture in which the scholar works. There is "personal involvement" without the problems of personalism. The scholar is moved and influenced by his material. He is not in control of it; it has him enveloped in *its* mystery. It leads him into unknown areas, pointing to his unconsciousness and opening up areas of his material formerly hidden. Remaining in an anima style of wonder, the scholar can then convey these mysteries imagistically without translating them into the known, rational, animus categories of thought so prized by usual scholarship. Without anima, scholarship has no soul and lacks a mode of being tethered to persons and to the cultural psyche as they attempt to work through their fate.

Jung and Hillman both speak of anima and animus as a syzygy. They appear as a tandem but not necessarily always in partnership. They can appear in a schizoid pattern so that one works against the other. For example, it is typical of scholarship when faced with images from art or religion to apply a rigorous animus analysis intended to force out some meaning. The capacity of the image to suffuse consciousness is lost in favor of an induced birth of meaning. On the other hand, anima can get in the way of the serious business of research by means of moods, fears, distractions and attachments that might foster imagination and feeling but do not serve scholarship. In the area of religion the split appears as animus dominance in religion scholarship and anima obsession in the practice of religion. Scholarship lacks soul in its attention to precise interpretations and studies, while the practice of religion often goes bereft of all critical sense. Religion, the patient, is deeply split, schizoid, in need of healing.

Jung defines anima in the language of interiority or inwardness. To speak of an anima type of scholarship in the area of religion, then, is to suggest an inward reading of images. It may not seem difficult to recommend inwardness in the study of religion, since religion itself has so much to say about what we call interior experience, but scholarship is almost exclusively external in its concerns. Scholarship is extraverted and prides itself on its extraversion, as if such an attitude assured a higher degree of reliability and substance. Scholarship is wary of anything that is not external, visible, measurable, and repeatable. As Jung says, "Extraversion goes hand in hand with mistrust of the inner man."9

An introverted study of religion, characterized by qualities of anima, would be less interested in arriving at factual information or at new analytical schemas and systems than in being moved in imagination. Like the feminine, imagination is much talked about but little used as a mode of study and exploration. Anima does not make the unknown known; rather, it provides an entry into unconsciousness or imagination. Anima does not translate images into concepts; it "dreams the dream onward" by remaining in the mode of images. Image-language evokes reflection and wonder. It moves consciousness deeper, more into ambiguities than beyond them, yet it is a language that has its own kind of precision and value. Kathleen Raine makes a similar point:

> Poetry Shelley defines as the language of
> imagination; a language not of definitions
> which measure, but of images which evoke,

knowledge; meaningless to the positivist, this language is, in relation to 'facts of mind,' exact.10

This image-language is precise in that it retains complexity and is close to the originating experience.

Jung's fundamental contribution to the study of religion is the manner in which he turns the language and phenomena of religion away from culture-bound belief systems toward the life of the psyche. In his commentary on the Tibetan Book of the Dead he makes it clear that he views analysis of religious language as though it were literal as archaic and outmoded:

> The Bardo Thodol is in the highest degree psychological in its outlook; but with us, philosophy and theology are still in the medieval, pre-psychological stage where only the assertions are listened to, explained, defended, criticized and disputed, while the authority that makes them has, by general consent, been deposed as outside the scope of discussion. Metaphysical assertions, however, are statements of the psyche and therefore are psychological.11

Religious phenomena, for Jung, reflect the syndromes, pathologies, movements, obstacles, longings, and various patterns that give psychological experience, whether individual or collective, its tone and shape. This is not to reduce religion to a personalistic psychology, but to "hear" religious language as speech about the soul, and not just the body.

Scholarship in religious studies does not appear nearly as connected to the life of people as research in other fields, such as medicine and psychology. Some religion scholars realize this and in response try to make their work more relevant. But to bring anima into religious studies is not to search for relevance or to apply the product of research to individual lives. Anima scholarship speaks to the soul of the person or of the society. That is to say, it offers reflection for the deep feelings and sufferings endured so often without a deep sense of significance or direction. Anima reflection does not explain, but it does offer guidance, substance, and a sense of shape or design.

One of Hillman's striking contributions to psychological thought is exactly a valuing of anima styles of reflection. In his Archetypal Psychology it is of great value to the psyche to find depth, to intensify questioning without answers, to engage in labyrinthine reflection, to come upon surprising perspectives, and to remain in the bowels of confusion to become familiar therein with directions and contours that are appropriate to psychological movement. In Hillman's view it is a spiritual concern to find answers and arrive at explanations. It is more appropriate to the psyche to remain in the mists, the twists of meaning, and the suggestiveness that psychological experience typically offers.

While it is true that the psychological level of understanding advocated by both Jung and Hillman does not imply an application of knowledge to particular cases; nevertheless, religious studies might move closer to an anima style by exploring the possibilities of a "practicum" dimension in the discipline. Research and theoretical studies in psychology, for example, obviously have their counterpart in psychotherapy. Ordinarily we think of religion's practicum as church worship, even when theoretical studies move away from literal belief and tend toward a more comparative analysis. Scholars who are not connected to a traditional religious institution have lost the advantages of the practicum: its concreteness, its proximity to experience, the immediate puzzles and mysteries it presents daily.

Revisioning the praxis derived from religious studies would go hand in hand with increased anima sensitivity in the study itself. Scholarship would find religious forms as an inherent part of all human life, whether or not those forms have an institutional context. The institutionalization of religious forms may be seen as a form of memory, a reminder of the religious patterns in all of life. Ritual is part of everyday life for everyone. A person is always living a myth: certain persons carrying the weight of mythic figures, certain places and events of crucial and formative importance to the psyche. Every day a person makes gestures, confesses, sacrifices, expresses contrition, communes with his friends, prepares for death, decides his morality, lives on what he believes. Religion is deeply quotidian. The religion scholar, freed from the literalism and scientism with which these forms are set apart from the quotidian and from the deeply personal and human, might be able to speak more __practically__, in the best sense of the word, to society and to individuals about these matters which, unreflected, are left to the religious opportunistic literalists, or are simply neglected. This kind of religion praxis is not going on except in those gray areas between psychology and religion touched upon perhaps by psychologists who have to deal with religious matters in the course of therapy, or by representatives of religion in their own forms of counseling. But even these occasions are not the practicum suggested here; for religion is as much a part of ordinary life as is psychology. Psychologists are concerned with ritual, sacrifice and confession, but they do not deal with them professionally as matters of religion. Religion scholars, on the other hand, tend to keep these forms within the settings of tradition and fail to explore them adequately as patterns of ordinary life.

When Jung reads the imagery of the Roman Catholic Mass as the process by which a person becomes an individual,12 when David Miller elaborates the Christian image of the Good Shepherd and warns about the dangerous tendency of any of us to be "sheepish,"13 and when James Hillman laments the reputed death of Pan as society's loss of instinct and surrender to panic,14 these soul-minded theologians are reflecting on religious issues in modern life by means of traditional religious images. These patterns are not so specifically psychological as they are religious. To consider the modern obsession with sexuality as a failure to be initiated into Aphrodite, or, with Rafael Lopez-Pedraza, to see sexual confusion and fascination for freakishness as a problem with Priapus,15 is to investigate the failure of religious awareness in modern life. This kind of theorizing suggests a practicum by which society and individuals might be guided through their religious confusion and suffering. Psychology and religion are clearly quite close at this point, but it is also clear that psychotherapists need help in understanding and responding to psychotic ritualism and to the myths they hear frequently from their patients. The society as a whole needs to deepen its understanding of religion so that it is no longer either dismissed as anachronistic or projected in a host of literalisms.

Theologians of the psyche--Jung, Miller, Hillman, Pedraza--have themselves turned to the poets of the

Pedraza--have themselves turned to the poets of the classical age and of the modern era to learn afresh the focus of religious sensibility. Poetry is the speech of the anima; therefore, it would be to the advantage of the religion scholar to recover a poetic rhetoric. According to Pedraza rhetoric is not an incidental matter of style, it is of the essence.16 Our modes of analysis will either miss or capture the anima side of consciousness. With the appropriate rhetoric, close to the poetic, mythic, and ritualistic style of the material of our study, we might reflect more deeply on the religious concerns of modern life. Entering the anima style, we could bring a sense of soul to our work, recovering thereby, without literalism, an ancient notion of religion itself: care of soul, _cura animae_.

NOTES

1. C. G. Jung, _Two Essays on Analytical Psychology_, trans. R. F. C. Hull, _Collected Works_, Vol. 7 (Princeton: Princeton University Press, 1966), pp. 192, 205, 299.

2. C. G. Jung, _Psychological Types_, revision by R. F. C. Hull of H. G. Baynes translation, _Collected Works_, Vol. 6 (Princeton: Princeton University Press, 1971), pp. 467f.

3. C. G. Jung, _Alchemical Studies_, trans. R. F. C. Hull, _Collected Works_, Vol. 13 (Princeton: Princeton University Press, 1967), p. 42.

4. _Ibid._

5. C. G. Jung, _Mysterium Coniunctionis_, trans. R. F. C. Hull, _Collected Works_, Vol. 14 (Princeton: Princeton University Press, 1970), p. 380.

6. _Ibid._

7. James Hillman, "Anima: II," in _Spring 1974_ (New York: Spring Publications, 1974), p. 126.

8. James Hillman, "Anima," in _Spring 1973_ (New York: Spring Publications, 1973), pp. 73, 128.

9. C. G. Jung, _Psychology and Religion: West and East_, trans. R. F. C. Hull, _Collected Works_, Vol. 11 (Princeton: Princeton University Press, 1969), p. 492.

10. Kathleen Raine, "Introduction," in _Thomas Taylor the Platonist_ (Princeton: Princeton University Press, 1969), p. 6.

11. C. G. Jung, _Collected Works_, Vol. 11, p. 492.

12. C. G. Jung, "Transformation Symbolism in the Mass," _Collected Works_, Vol. 11, pp. 203-96.

13. David L. Miller, _Christs_ (New York: The Seabury Press, 1981), Part One.

14. James Hillman, "An Essay on Pan," in _Pan and the Nightmare_ (Zurich: Spring Publications, 1972).

15. Rafael Lopez-Pedraza, _Hermes and His Children_ (Zürich: Spring Publications, 1977).

16. _Ibid._, pp. 125-131.

CHAPTER 11

IRELAND: LAND OF ETERNAL YOUTH

Walter and Mary Brenneman

From the perspective of the history and
phenomenology of religion, the psychological findings
of Jung function as a microcosmic parallel to the
religious patterns found in the world at large.
Because of this parallel relationship, it is possible
to apply the findings of Jung and his circle to
situations occurring in the great world," using them
as a tool of interpretation. It is just such a
methodological technique that we have employed in the
study of Irish Celtic myth. In short, this amounts to
the interpretation of myth by the use of myth, that
is, we let the myth become its own interpretation, we
allow it to remain mythic.

In the course of our study, we found that Irish
myth was motivated by the relationship of the Goddess
to her sons and to her consort, the Lord of the
Otherworld. We were struck by the congruence of this
pattern to that of Jung's notion of the _puer aeternus_
and his relationship to the old king, the _senex_, which
is dominated or oriented by the Mother Goddess. The
problem that arises in this relationship, both
mythically and psychologically, is that the old king
resists succession by his son, and in doing so evolves
into the rigid Lord of Death. In other words, the
senex and the _puer_ are separated. Resolution consists
of the son redeeming his father by use of the magical
weapons gained in the Otherworld through the Mother.
The "defeat" of the father by the son through the
Mother renews the world.

In expanding the psychological theme of the _puer_

176

into the macrocosm of Irish myth, we discovered that the context of the puer, his place of being, is the Otherworld. The Otherworld is a curious combination of death and life, for it is a place in which the dead dwell, yet their visage is eternally youthful and their life eternally happy. This death/life paradox is made possible because of the location of the Otherworld at the very edge of the world, on the boundary. Names for the Otherworld such as the "western isles," "land of youth," "plain of pleasure," and "land of ever living women" give us a sense of the paradox of which we speak, but it is the western location of the Otherworld that caught our attention. This western extremity is identified over and over with the Otherworld,1 and prior to the European discovery of America, Ireland herself was the western most place. This island, therefore, was identified by the Celts who arrived there as the Otherworld.

The Otherworld, then, is the highly sought after land of eternal youth and beautiful women at the western boundary of the world. Ireland functioned as this place until the movement farther west by the Europeans and the establishment of a new paradise, a new dwelling place for the puer aeternus, his Mother and his terrible father, the senex. Based upon the methodological principal of parallels stated above, it now becomes clear that Ireland's mythos may be taken as a paradigm for the cultural psyche of the west.

In order to pursue these insights, we researched simultaneously into the psychology of the puer and Irish myths involving kingship succession and the relationship of the king to the Goddess, Ireland. Within the extant research on the puer archetype we found a considerable division in emphasis between Jung and M. L. von Franz on the one hand and James Hillman on the other. The Jungian camp saw the puer as "motherbound," and needing to free himself from this bind. The Hillmanians, however, saw the puer as bound by the father, the need being to free himself by means of his redemption or "defeat" of the senex with the aid of occult insight gained through intimacy with the mother.

For Jung the puer presents us with another version of the male problem of individuation from the unconscious, identified by Jung with the Mother. There is almost no reference to the puer's relationship with his father such as we find in his

177

discussion of the hero. He speaks rather of the puer aeternus as a mother's son who is so delicate because of his dependence upon her that he dies an early death. He has no sense of reality and lives encased within a cocoon of fantasy. "The graceful Baldur is such a figure," Jung writes. "This type is granted only a fleeting existence, because he is never anything but an anticipation of something desired or hoped for. . . . The reason is that he only lives on and through the mother and can strike no roots in the world, so that he finds himself in a state of permanent incest."2 M. L. von Franz amplifies Jung's position when she states that: "With the concept of the eternal youth, puer aeternus, we in psychology describe a definite form of neurosis in men, which is distinguished by a fixation (Steckenbleiben) in the age of adolescence as a result of an all too strong mother-bind."3

For Hillman, however, the puer does not define himself over against the mother but as over against the old father or senex. To be sure, the son is in need of individuation from the unconscious, but this individuation is swallowed by the father who devours his sons, not by the mother who actually provides him with magical aid in surpassing or redeeming the senex. Hillman states: "We would differentiate puer, hero, and son, and contrary to the classical analytical view, we would suggest that the son who succumbs and the hero who overcomes both take their definition through the relationship with the magna mater, whereas the puer takes its definition from the senex-puer polarity."4 This is not to say that the puer has no relationship with the mother, but it is a positive relationship rather than an antagonistic one. Hillman notes that "The Goddess even encourages the puer ambition and is instrumental to senex-puer reunion."5 What is lacking in the puer who is separated from the senex is the ability to discriminate and to be a father. In his conflict with the senex, he renews the kingship with his youth while at the same time taking on the father role, that is, he becomes king. This act of redemption is a mutual sacrifice in which the puer sacrifices his youthful vision to the senex and the senex his discrimination to the puer.

It is Hillman's interpretation of the puer aeternus that provided the most insight into the Irish tales and myths of so-called heroes. For, in every case, we saw a son who had a special relationship with

178

his mother, and in fact, was protected by her against the destructive desires of his father. The son was taken by her to the Otherworld to avoid destruction by the father. After the mother trained him in magical warfare, he returned to do battle with the senex and in victory, took on the kingship.

In order to clarify the working out of this pattern and its influence upon a revisioned understanding of the west, we must first look at the Irish/Celtic cosmogony, cosmology, so-called hero tales and kingship rituals. The general Celtic theme of cosmogony is that of a watery creation, or a creation which, in Mircea Elaide's terms is cosmic at base and is grounded in symbols of the feminine.6 It is the flood which creates the world, which, according to Jean Markale,7 often results in a submerged city/world. This theme is present in the tale of Ys, a twelfth century text of Graelent-Meur, attributed to Marie de France, in which King Grandlon of Cornwall returns from a war in the north with a beautiful Nordic fairy queen. She bears a baby girl, born of the sea, and dies in childbirth. The child, Dahut, is raised by Grandlon who builds a city for her on low ground, near the sea, and surrounded by a dike. Grandlon is converted to Christianity while Dahut remains pagan. St. Gwennole visits Gradlon and warns of the imminent destruction of the city. The king and his retinue leave just as a great storm appears and the city is flooded. Dahut perishes in the flood with her "father's" key about her neck. The city is now established as the Otherworld. The most prominent Irish version is the myth of Cessair's voyage to Ireland and her subsequent destruction by flood. This myth plays an important part in the Irish Cosmogony.

Another Irish variant comes from the Leabhar na huidre. Here a sacred spring or well is guarded by a magical maiden. She is neglected and the spring overflows, drowning the old king. The king's daughter, Libane, escapes and lives under Lough Neagh for a year. She is transformed into a salmon, and three hundred years later is baptized in human form as the goddess Morrigan, or, "born of the sea."8

We find the same pattern of the lady at the well in a Welsh version in which a drunkard in search of water to quench his thirst, comes upon a sacred spring guarded by a lovely maiden whom he rapes.9 The spring overflows and floods the world. In all versions, the

179

spring or sea is identified with the lovely maiden. Her relationship with the king or drunkard must be understood as an act of fertilization, through which the spring overflows and the world is reborn. It is the Mother goddess whose vaginal spring is the source of creation both for the cosmos and for humankind.

The cosmological structure of Ireland bears out these suggestions still further. If we look at this structure from the perspective of our sky-oriented cosmology, it appears to be inverted, for power radiates from the bottom up rather than from the top down. In other words, the "Otherworld" or underworld, is the primary power source and contains the models or archetypes for the surface world. The surface world is a reflection of the Otherworld and is dependent upon the Otherworld queen for its sustenance. The sky is of secondary importance and is, due to its distance from the source of power, an ephemeral reality. The Otherworld is the embodiment of the great goddess and is her belly or womb. In it are contained the archetypal talismans which convey power from their source in the goddess and which sustain and recreate the world. Of these talismans the most important is the well of Segais, for it is this well which is identified with the cosmogonic wells of the tales previously mentioned.10 This well is also identified with he vagina of the Goddess Ireland, who is both the well and its guardian.11 Her mating with her son/lover/king (i.e., symbolized by his drinking from the well) who journeys to her from the surface world, brings about the recreation of Ireland and the establishment of kingship. The other talismans of the Otherworld are: the sword that never fails, the spear that never misses its mark, the stone of wisdom, and the cauldron that never runs empty. The magical weapons in this group are forged in the belly of the goddess by the Lord of the Otherworld, consort to the Goddess, Otherworld sun, and father or grandfather to the surface king.12

The Otherworld is the land of eternal youth, "The Land of Promise," "The Plain of Delights" and the "Land of Ever Living Women." It was also the site of the eternal banquet whose fare was the goddess, and whose host was her husband, "The Lord of the Otherworld," the divine smithy.13 It was at this banquet that the mating of the maiden at the well and the earthly king took place, before the well, its sacred tree, or bile, and the cauldron and magic

180

weapons.

The so-called "hero" tales of Ireland reflect this ritual and clarify the pattern of the puer, his relationship to his mother, and his antagonism and redemptive function toward his father.14 There are two major variations to this pattern in Irish myth. The first is that of the young man who is sought to be killed by his father. The mother of the child takes him away to a foreign land, e.g. Alba, which symbolizes the Otherworld. There he is raised in secret by his mother, learns to fight, and ultimately returns to slay the present king, his father, and assume his rightful place as king. The most typical of these tales is that of Tuathal Techtmar,15 whose father is slain by Ellim mac Corach. His mother, daughter of the king of Alba, flees to Alba, and there gives birth to Tuathal whom she raises in secret for twenty years. She then accompanies him back to Ireland where he defeats the present king and assumes the kingship. In the second variant the son is in contest with the lord of the Otherworld and kills him.16 The otherworld god is his father or grandfather, and by killing him, the son assumes the role of Lord of the Otherworld, host of the otherworld feast and consort of the Goddess, his mother. Here again we see the theme of puer aeternus, who is raised by the mother in her belly, and who emerges to redeem the senex Lord of the Otherworld and becomes consort of the Goddess. This variant is present in the tales of Cuchulainn, who is taught the art of battle in the underworld by the goddess Scathach, ultimately to emerge and defeat the Lord of the Otherworld, Goll mac Garbada.17 The same theme is seen in the myth of Lug and his battle with Baler, champion of the monsterous race of the Fomorians. Here Lug, the youthful sun god is given the magical weapons of the otherworld smithies Goibniu, Luchta and Credne. With these weapons he defeats Baler, ancient Lord of the Otherworld sun.18

In all these myths, the puer is associated with the sun in the sky, the secondary sun, whereas his father/grandfather is the sun under the earth, the primary sun. As underworld sun the father/grandfather is the smithie who forges (in the forge of the earth) the weapon used by the puer to kill him. This is the lightning weapon, the sword of intuitive wisdom born of the mother, but like unto the father. With this weapon the puer "kills" or replaces the old Lord of the Otherworld thereby mating with his mother, the well of the world. Through this union, the life giving waters of the well overflow and the world is renewed along with the kingship. The _puer_ now becomes father, Lord, and the ritual is complete.

In the rituals of pagan Irish kings, the imagery of the well and of the contest of the son with the father are conjoined. The central ritual of kingship is that of coronation, or the process of the attainment and assumption of the role of king. Kingship was not necessarily passed on from father to son, although the succession could remain within the same family for as long as that family was able to retain sovereignty, or favor with the goddess, Ireland. A king could mate with any number of women beside his mortal wife, and any of the sons of these unions were eligible for the kingship. Thus, the challengers to the old king, the _puer_ figures, were numerous.

Ritually, as the virility of the old king waned, so did the fecundity of the goddess, Ireland. She was transformed gradually from a beautiful maiden at the well to an old hag. This ritual paradigm, presented mythically in "The Five Sons of Eochaidh" found in the _Temair Breg_, runs as follows. The old king is waning and the five sons go in turn to a sacred well (presumably located at the inauguration site) to drink of the water and thus to gain wisdom, sovereignty and kingship over Ireland. The well is guarded by a most hideous hag who demands from each a kiss before she will grant the draught of sacred water in the goblet which is a symbol of the well and their union. The water is sacred because it provides hidden wisdom. It is intoxicating and often described as ale.19 Each of the brothers refuses until the last and youngest, Niall, arrives. When she makes the request of him, he throws his arms about her "as if she were forever his wife."20 At this moment she is transformed into a beautiful maiden and foretells his rule at Tara.

In this myth we see the coming together of the two themes of the _puer_'s incest relationship with this mother and his victory over his aging father, the _senex_. At the moment the hag is transformed into a beautiful maiden through her union with her son, the old king lets go of his kingship, he dies and by means of his death is unified with or redeemed by the _puer_. The simultaneity of these events in the myth are lived

182

The simultaneity of these events in the myth are lived out in time through the constant challenges to the father/king which are brought to him by his many sons. At length, through his weakness, his loss of virility, he "lets go" and the water of the well is drunk by the victorious son at the ensuing inauguration ritual. This ritual marks the union of the son to the father for the son in becoming king is now father, but only because of the magical powers granted to him by the mother. A quote from the Annals of the Four Masters makes clear that the kingship was passed on through the killing of the old king by the new:

    i   Finn reigned twenty two years and was killed by Setna

    ii Setna reigned twenty years and was killed by Siomon the Freckled

    iii Siomon reigned six years and was killed by Dui son of Siomon

    iv Dui reigned ten years and was killed by Muiredach son of Dui

    v   Muiredach reigned one year and was killed by Enna son of Muiredach 21

The myth of "The Five Sons of Eochaidh" presents us with the ritual context of this murder. T. G. E. Powell corroborates our interpretation when he states:

> there can be little doubt that the Celtic king, in fully pagan times at least, met a violent but ritual end, and there are a number of somewhat veiled allusions to deaths by weapon wounds, drowning and burning, in the midst of high magic, in the presence of the hag and the tribal god.22

The inauguration ritual, then, took place at the well around which the prospective king, having been identified as the sun/son by the scream of the stone of Ireland, lia fal, circumambulates sunwise. He is then granted the goblet of "ale" (water from the sacred well). Upon drinking the ale he is simultaneously united with the goddess (he takes her in, she becomes immanent with him), becomes sovereign and imagination of the _puer_ which is made possible by the magic of the mother, the holy well.

With the coming of St. Patrick to Ireland sometime in the latter fourth century,23 the early Celtic soteriological model which we have put forth seems to move from the _puer_ redeeming _senex_ to a hero who slays mother. The hero's task is to conquer the dragon and dispose of the underworld. Patrick's world is a surface world, dependent upon the overworld; _sky_, the father in heaven, provides the sustenance rather than mother. The sacred wells are a central problem for Patrick as he races about24 re-allocating power, territorializing, and purifying those wells in the name of the father. The underworld is to be dried up like the desert.

Patrick's cosmogony is a fiery one. This image appears long before his missionary tenure in Ireland.25 The tripartate life of Patrick tells us that:

> At his foster mother's, the roof leaked. It was cold and Patrick was whining for food. Said his step-mother, "this is not what distresses us! There is something we would do rather than make food for thee, when not even the fire is alive." Patrick then dipped his hand into the water and from the five drops flowing from Patrick's fingers sparks appeared and the fire blazed up.26

Another time he brings "a lap-ful of icicles" to his foster mother who admonishes him that "to bring a faggot of fire wood that we might warm ourselves would be better than what thou hast brought." At which point little Patrick made the icicles "flame like firewood."27

Both legends demonstrate the early powers of transformation which Patrick was said to possess, and the employment of those powers with flame through which he turns chaos, which he sees as cold, wet and withholding, into order, dryness, and warmth. In later years, Patrick uses this same power to de-feminize or cauterize the wells, the Celtic symbol of regeneration.

The celestial nature of Patrick's staff and Patrick's intention of serving the sky god are made clear in the manner in which he obtains his staff. Shortly after he arrived as a missionary in Ireland he went to Mt. Hermon where the Lord gave him "the magic staff of Jesus."28 Then Patrick, in his Druidic white robes,29 strode about Ireland, striking into wells with his staff, thus bringing about their transformation from fecundating pagan wells serving the mother, into cleansing, pure, 'sained' wells, whose water blesses those in the service to the God in heaven. As Patrick blesses the wells with the staff of God, he is in imitation of Moses. He, also, spent forty days in the desert. It is said that Patrick died at age 120, as a dessicated old man, having climbed the mountain, and having cast out the serpents, thus defeating the feminine and creating a sky-oriented order.

Patrick is now guardian of the wells, and as he sits at dawn by the well Cliabach on the side of Cruachan, the inauguration site at Connacht, King Lowgairs's twin daughters appear. Ruddy and fair, they address the white-robed assembly: "Whence are ye, and whence have ye come? Are ye of the elves or of the gods?" St. Patrick describes his god, and attracts the girls, who receive the baptism. Then they express a wish to see Jesus, face to face. Patrick answers: "Ye cannot see Christ unless ye first taste of death" at which point, "they receive the sacrifice and sleep in death."30 Then the princesses are buried at that place. So now the girls, rather than the young men, as previously, are sacrificed to the sky god through the now-transformed well.

Another image involving Patrick and the feminine is seen in the justice he metes out to Liapat, his sister and faithful follower when she begs forgiveness for a sexual transgression. He simply rides over her in his chariot, and, when he looks back and sees her still supplicating, bloodied, on her knees in the road, commands his driver to drive over her twice more until she is dead.31 Surely this is paternal rage. The image is compounded when we learn that Patrick was once married to her by his slave father, but rather than consummate the marriage, Patrick stayed up all night praying, and was rewarded, at the light of day when a small disfigurement on her forehead revealed that she was his long-lost sister sold into slavery. The image of Patrick's enslaved anima, indeed!

When Patrick is informed that ten virgins,

daughters of the Kings of Lombardy are proceeding in pilgrimage toward him, he suggests that "three of the virgins will go to heaven, and bury them in the place where they are" (a hazelwood); the rest go to the cliffs, and "let one of them go as far as this hillock."32 Patrick surely conquers the feminine! He slays women wherever necessary in order that the overworld rather than the underworld will give sustenance to the surface world. The water of the wells is transformed for service to the overworld by the staff of Patrick. The maidens are sacrificed to God. If they mate, they mate with God. Father orders and creates the world, not the mother. Patrick as father, and for father, creates the world. His staff is his talisman, and his method is dissolution of the underworld. But is Patrick a hero, or is he a negative *senex* figure? Has Patrick's cauterization of the wells made the acceptance of his sons an impossibility? Perhaps the following tale will clarify the question. Prior to receiving his staff on Mt. Hermon, Patrick saw a withered old woman on her hands and knees, who is in the company of an eternally young couple. "What is it that the hag is?" saith Patrick: "Great is her feebleness." "She is a grand-daughter of mine" saith the young man. And he then explains that they have been blessed with eternal life, without decay and have a staff, the gift of god, for Patrick. "I will not take it," saith Patrick, "til He, himself gives me his staff."33

By refusing to take the staff of the hag, Patrick accepts the role of the *senex* and denies the eternal youths, the *puer aeternae,* as well as loses his own possibility for redemption. Patrick functions as the ancient Irish king, but is unwilling to give himself up and to accept his sons *through* the feminine mysteries occurring at the well.

To this day Patrick's legacy, the church, in the republic of Ireland assumes the role of *senex,* withered father, rather than its traditional role as mother. The women of Ireland have remained in service to the church, obedient to the father/priest. The men stand separated, often at the rear of the church during mass, and leave immediately afterward to imbibe the ale of the goddess in the dark well of the pub. Men pledge to the death in obedience to the IRA, while the boys give themselves over and over as eternal sacrifices to "Her," the emerald that is Ireland.

Ireland thus remains a model for the west. In its placehood it is a microcosm for the idea of the west and presents an archetype for an understanding of ourselves and the dis-ease of the west. Hillman's work provides a model for understanding that so long as the mother, the well, remains cauterized, the sacrifice of the _puer_/sons will not be accepted by the _senex_. The dis-ease of the West is not in its failure to slay the dragon, but in its inability to unite father and son _through_ the acceptance of the mediating mother.

NOTES

1. Mythologically, the earliest references to
   Ireland and the west as "other" is found in the
   myth of the invasion of Cessair located in the
   Lebhar Gabhala which is a part of the 12th
   century Book of Leinster. Cessair was the
   granddaughter of Noah who seeks to escape the
   flood. Noah refuses her and her company a place
   on the ark and advises her to "go forthe unto the
   most western borders of the world, for the flood
   will assuredly not come there." Seven years
   later she arrived as the first invader to the
   shores of Ireland. The seventh century scholar
   Giraldus Cambresis in his Topographia Hibernica
   Dist. III, chap. 1, describes the same myth. ".
   . . Caesara, a granddaughter of Noah, hearing
   that the flood was near at hand, resolved to
   escape by sailing with her companions to the
   farthest islands of the west, . . . hoping that,
   where sin had never been committed, the flood,
   its avenger, would not come." Even within
   Ireland herself, the western extremities are more
   powerful and associated with both death and
   eternal youth. The province of Munster is
   identified with the Otherworld due to its
   south-western location, and still more the House
   of Donn and the world of the dead lie off the
   west coast of west Munster (A. and B. Rees,
   Celtic Heritage, Thames and Hudson, London, 1961,
   pp. 134-136.)

2. C. G. Jung, Collected Works, vol. 5, Bollingen
   Series XX, (Princeton, New Jersey: Princeton
   University Press, 1956), p. 258.

3. M. L. von Franz, "Ueber religiose Hintergrunde
   des Puer-Aeternus-Problems," The Archetype, ed.
   A. Guggenbuhl-Craig (Basel: Karger, 1964), p.
   141.

4. James Hillman, "The Great Mother, Her Son, Her
   Hero, and the Puer," Fathers and Mothers, ed. P.
   Berry (Zurich: Spring Publications, 1973), p.
   76.

5. _Ibid_.

6. See Mircea Eliade, _Patterns in Comparative Religion_ (New York: The World Publishing Company, 1963), no. 61 "Water Cosmogonies" and no. 62 "Water as Universal Mother."

7. The material in the flood cosmogony is gathered from Jean Markale's _Celtic Civilization_ (London and New York: Gordon and Cremonesi, 1978), chap. 1.

8. _Ibid_., p. 23.

9. _Ibid_., p. 24.

10. See A. and B. Rees, _Celtic Heritage_, p. 161.

11. Jean Markale, _Celtic Civilization_, p. 24.

12. See T. F. O'Rahilly, _Early Irish History and Mythology_, Dublin Institute for Advanced Studies, Dublin, 1964, p. 60ff.

13. _Ibid_., p. 121-122.

14. _Ibid_., p. 326.

15. See O'Rahilly pp. 154-159 for this tale and the important role played by the Mother in Tuathal's attaining of kingship.

16. _Ibid_., p. 278. The Lord of the Otherworld and the old kings are symbolically identical and function as _senex_ in the _senex-puer_ polarity.

17. See Thomas Kinsella trans., _The Tain_ (London: Oxford University Press, 1969).

18. See Myles Dillon, _Early Irish Literature_ (Chicago: University of Chicago Press, 1948), pp. 58-62.

19. We see the water of the well described as ale in the tale "The Phantom's Frenzy" in which the maiden of the well, seated upon a crystal throne, prophesies to Conn the future kings of Ireland. With each prophesy she pours out a goblet of ale as the name is spoken.

20. See S. H. O'Grady, Silva Gadelica (London: Williams & Norgate, 1892), I, 327-330 and II, 369-373, 489-548 for this tale and those concerning the hagat and the well.

21. See John O'Donovan, The Annals of the Four Masters, 2nd edition (Dublin: Hodges, Smith & Company, 1856), V. 3, p. 56.

22. T. G. E. Powell, The Celts (London: Thames and Hudson, 1958), pp. 121-122.

23. Whitley Stokes ed., Rerum Brittannicarum Medii AEVI scriptores, The Tripartite Life of Patrick, London, 1887, p. cxxxiii.

24. A cursory skimming of The Tripartite Life will give the reader an idea of the peripatetic nature of this mission.

25. There are very few truths about Patrick. Born in the Britains, he was enslaved at age 16, taken to Ireland where he herded swine for six years, ran away, did a desert journey, returned to Britain, had a dream that he should return to Ireland, and after a time in Italy, returned as an old man, to convert the pagans.

26. Whitley Stokes, p. 11.

27. Ibid.

28. Book of Armagh, fo. 14, a. 1.

29. The Rawlinson Collection, Catalogi codicum manuscriptorum Bibliothecae Bodleiana Partis Quintao Casciculus Primis, Oxanii: 1862, col. 728-732, B., 512, fo. 12, a. 2.

30. Translation from Latin of Book of Armagh by Dr. Todd in Life of St. Patrick, Dublin, 1864, pp. 453-455.

31. The Rawlinson Collection, B., 512, fo. 27, a. 1, vs. 20-25.

32. Ibid., vs. 10-15.

33. Egerton Manuscript 93, trans. 1781 of Pope Innocent's treatise De miseria humanae

<u>conditionis,</u> fo. 2, a. 1, vs. 15-30.

CHAPTER 12

IN THE MIDDLE OF A DARK WAY

The _descensus_ _ad_ _inferos_ in C. G. Jung and James
Hillman

David L. Miller

> "In the middle, not only
>   in the middle of the way
> But all the way, in a dark
>   wood, in a bramble,
> On the edge of a grimpen,
>   where is no secure foothold
> . . . .
> Which shall be the darkness
>   of God."
>   --T. S. Eliot

Although modern religious women and men in
America seem reticent to pronounce the phrase
descendit _ad_ _inferos_ when piously intoning the
Christian creed, Sigmund Freud and secular depth
psychologists following in Freud's wake, like numerous
ancient Gnostics, have seemed eager to liken the
journey of the self in this world to an underworldly
descent. The point is summed in advance by Freud who
takes his motto for _The_ _Interpretation_ _of_ _Dreams_ from
Virgil's _Aeneid_: _Flectere_ _si_ _nequeo_ _superos,_ _Acheronta_
movebo, "If I cannot bend the higher powers, I will
move Acheron."

Perhaps one could imagine this old saying as
motto, not only to a single book, but to the whole
variety of recent interactions between depth

psychology and religion, noting as a sort of test case for the permutations of this interaction differing perspectives on the _descensus ad inferos_. More particularly to the instance of the present essay, there is the case of an important difference between C. G. Jung and James Hillman on the psychological referent of the motif of "descent into hell," and this difference symbolizes a larger difference between these two concerning the relation of psychology to religion, especially the Christian religion.

An examination of this particular difference may hopefully serve to demonstrate the matter of "depths" of psyche which may be at once seen as "the darkness of God," concerning which not only Eliot, but also Nietzsche and many others have spoken. Such, at least, is the intuition and effort of this essay. First, then, to the descent in Jung . . .

C. G. Jung

In the Index to the Collected Works of Jung, there are twenty-eight entries listed under the three headings of "_descensus ad inferos_," "_descensus_," and "Christ--descent into Hell." Typical of this more than a score of uses is the reference Jung makes in the lectures he gave at the Tavistock Clinic in the Autumn of 1935 when he was almost sixty years old. He is explaining to physicians in Great Britain his notion of "archetype," citing St. Augustine's similar use of the term. Jung observes that certain non-subjective or transpersonal patterns appear in fantasy, dream, and behavior. One such imaginal structure, he says, "is the Katabasis, the Descent into the Cave, the Nekyia." Jung goes on:

> You remember in the Odyssey where Ulysses descends _ad inferos_ to consult Tiresias, the seer. The motif of the Nekyia is found everywhere in antiquity and practically all over the world.[1]

This archetypal image, Jung suggests, is a sort of meta-archetype, an archetype of the notion of archetype in depth psychology, since "it expresses the psychological mechanism of introversion of the conscious mind into the deeper layers of the unconscious psyche."[2] Among the many images resident in Jung's psychological ideas, the _descensus ad inferos_, then, is a crucial one.

It is also likely not without significance that exactly half of Jung's references to the *descensus* (i.e., fourteen) are linked to alchemy and its symbolism. More specifically, the *descensus* of the self into the depths is likened to the particular "stage" of *nigredo* in alchemical process. Jung utilizes the alchemical symbolism to describe that crucial stage of darkening and deepening, say in a depression, which begins the process of individuation. When one is "down," she or he feels and senses things that are unconscious when not "down." If there be no *descensus*, i.e., no *nigredo*, then there will be no *depth* psychology, no deep sense (*logos*) of the self (*psyche*).

The descent into the underworld taken from the tales of mythology is described by Jung in terms of the *nigredo* of alchemy. Both mythology and alchemy are taken as expressions of the darkening and deepening of the self's sense of itself, which in turn is spoken of in alchemy and mythology. *Obscurum per obscurius, ignotum per ignotius*--"the obscure by the more obscure, the unknown by the more unknown": such was Jung's hermeneutic principle.3 Psyche experiences itself as fantasy and image,4 so one ought keep to images in the psychologizing. A psychology of depth is a descent into deeper meanings, which means, imaginal meanings whose modality, by virtue of rich and polymorphic ambiguity, has depth in itself.

In addition to the alchemical associations, Jung uses the motif of *descensus* to refer explicitly to "Nekyia." Twenty of his uses, including some of the alchemical ones, refer to the mythological motif of the "night-sea journey." And six of these twenty mention the falling into the "belly" of a "whale" or "large fish." Often Jung means these motifs symbolically to refer to the psychological experience of becoming unconscious, and therefore being confronted with the task of making the unconscious more conscious; sometimes, however, Jung means his talk of the "descent" to refer to a "falling" into consciousness concerning something that was heretofore unconscious, thereby deepening the life-meaning with new shadings and nuancings.

This is all to say that Jung straightforwardly accepted a mythological and a Christian image--"the descent into hell"--as describing a psychological

194

"truth" or "reality" in a mode appropriate to the self's experience of that reality: _ignotium per ignotius_. This confirmation of a religious datum from the side of Jung's depth psychology is, however, compromised when one realizes that in order for, say, **Christ's** descent into hell to be psychologically useful, it had to be interpreted gnostically or alchemically, which is to say, "heretically." Man is the redeemer of the "gold" imprisoned in "lead," rather than being viewed as the "lead" to be redeemed by the "gold."5 The descent is from the psyche's pleromatic wholeness into the darkness of history's one-sidedness, rather than being a descent from historical "light" into mythic "darkness."

G. K. Chesterton once said, "orthodoxy is a reticence." Jung found orthodox interpretations of religious images and symbols to be, indeed, a psychological reticence, and though he was confirmatory of the motifs of religion, he was also confirmatory of the whole tradition of the interpretation of those motifs, heresy being a necessary therapy of theology's psychological onesidedness, a making whole of meanings which are so important to the lives of persons today, but which have too often been accompanied by perspectives which are partial.6

James Hillman

Where Jung is positive about the Christian notion of the _descesus ad inferos christi_, Hillman is negative. "Christianism," he writes, is a "barrier" to a depth-understanding of the self. And precisely the instance Hillman cites is Christ's "descent into the underworld." He quotes Tertullian as being in his view typical of dominant theology and popular piety: "Christ's descent was for this purpose . . . that we might not have to descend therein."7 Or again, Hillman writes: "Christ's mission to the underworld was to annul it. He exempts us from the descent."8

Psychologically, this "Christianism" in belief and culture functions to make us feel shame, guilt, and anxiety when we are "down." Christ saved us from _inferos_, or so Christian theology implies, so my feeling of being down must be my fault. Far from being an expression of our condition, an "explanation" _ignotius per ignotium_, Christ's descent is one more expression of an unrealistic "should" or "ought" which is precisely not therapeutic but productive of neurosis. Christianism, thereby, takes the depth out of our psychology, or at least it tries to do so.9

Like Jung, Hillman notes the psychological one-sidedness of dominant Christian interpretations of religious images; unlike Jung, Hillman rejects the Christian motifs and turns to Greek forms.10 Typical is Hillman's rhetoric in an Eranos lecture of 1968: "Do dreams belong to Moses and Jesus and Paul, or to Night and her children (Oneiroi, Hypnos, Thanatos, Old Age, and Fate) and Hades?"11 Jung wants Christian symbols revisioned psychologically; Hillman wants to re-vision psychology so as to save it from Christian dominance.

Hillman's reference to dreams at Eranos is important and marks another distinction between him and Jung on the motif of the _descensus_. Whereas Jung connects the _descensus_ to a stage in the process of individuation by way of the _nigredo_ of alchemy, Hillman's references to the _descensus ad inferos_ are more psyche-specific, having most often to do, not with psychological development wherever it may be experienced, but particularly with the experience of dream.

Hillman's book, _The Myth of Analysis_, was published first in 1972. It contained the lectures given at Eranos meetings in 1966, 1968, and 1969. Though there is no index-entry in this book to "descent" or "_descensus ad inferos_" or "underworld," there are five entries under the name "Hades," and they commonly indicate Hillman's counter-ascensionalism, i.e., that the access to spirit is by way of soul, rather than there being an access to soul by way of spirit.

By the time Hillman's 1972 Terry Lectures at Yale University were published as the book _Re-visioning Psychology_ (1975), the "underworld" had six index-entries and there was a major section dramatically placed at the book's end, a section called "Hades, Persephone, and a Psychology of Death." In this one can read: "In Hades' realm _psyche_ alone exists . . . from the Hades-perspective _we are our images_, i.e., (_eidola_)."12 It is clear that the motif of the descent into the underworld was becoming critical for Hillman, even though its Christic form was avoided.

That the experience of dream is the psychological
locus classicus of the descensus ad inferos was
asserted by Hillman at an Eranos lecture in 1973 even
before Re-visioning Psychology had been published.
The title of that lecture was "The Dream and the
Underworld," and the talk was expanded into a book and
was published under the same title in 1979. Here the
matter culminates. The entire book--on dream, on
therapeutic experience--is about the descensus ad
inferos. The index entries under "descent" and
"Nekyia" burgeon. What was imagined as a "stage" in
Jung is now clue to the deep experience of the whole;
but the crux is very particular. It is in looking at
dreams and in looking at life through dream.

In sum, then, the Christian symbol of the descent
of Christ into hell, for Jung, shows a stage we all
must go through; whereas, for Hillman, the Christian
version of the journey to the deeps shows an
experience we do not have to undergo since Christ did
it for us. Jung says: Yes. Hillman says: No.

But it would be easy to stress the differences
and neglect the essential sameness of Jung and
Hillman. For both agree that religious images, such
as the descensus ad inferos, refer to individual
experience, as well as to meta-physical matters. And
both psychologists want to deepen and darken Christian
meanings, Jung by revisioning it from the side of
repressed hermeneutics, and Hillman by rejecting it in
favor of another symbology (Greek) whose hermeneutic
is already more "whole" (i.e., polytheistically
pleromatic). As Hillman says: "To know the psyche at
its basic depths, for a true depth psychology, one
must go to the underworld."13 And Jung echoes in
advance: "It [the descensus] expresses the
psychological mechanism of the introversion of the
conscious mind into the deeper layers of the
unconscious."14

Whatever historical or eschatological meaning the
descensus ad inferos christi may have in theology,
referring to a historical event of the first Good
Friday or to an ultimate resurrection of those born
before Christ, this religious image can also be viewed
as a psychological truth about the real sense of
things here and now. Pious Christians may have
trouble with the saying, "he descended into hell," but
depth psychology, for all its variety, finds the

saying crucial to the understanding of life with depth. On this, in spite of their differences, Jung and Hillman are finally at one.

In the Middle

But there is yet a third view, between Jung and Hillman. It is a theological rather than a psychological view, yet it is a _descensus_-theology that also has implications for psychology, just as Jung's Yes and Hillman's No have implications for theology.

Theologically, the clue is the word "middle." The Catholic, Hans Urs von Balthasar, put the obvious matter forthrightly. Speaking of Christ's descent into hell, he said that it happened in the _mitte Zwischen Kreuz und Auferstehung_, "in the middle between the crucifixion and resurrection."15 The _descensus_ is in the "middle," as if to say that "being down" configures with "being between." Bousset, in his well-known study, _Kyrios Christos_, amplifies the matter further:

> The acceptance of the three-day interval between death and resurrection now opened a new door to Christian imagination. People did not stop with the simple idea of rest in the tomb or of the tarrying of the soul with the corpse. There developed the fantasy of the descent of Jesus into Hades.16

One German theologian (J. Pohle) goes so far as to imagine that the article on Christ's descent in the Creed came about, as he puts it, "through the need to answer the question about where Christ's soul could be in the time between death and resurrection."17 A French Catholic scholar seems to agree, saying, _Peut-etre l'article a-t-il precisement ete insere dans le Credo pour remplir cet hiatus._18

The point is clear. The theological imagination provokes the thought that "being down" comes after something has died and before a new life is realized: in the middle! A deep life is imagined as when one senses things as "between" or, as Tillich used to say, "on the boundary." This is, of course, all too familiar.

But it is not only "all too familiar" because of

life-experiences which corroborate this image and which this image articulates and figures. The "middle way" is also so familiar because it has so often been commended.

Heraclitus already spoke of God as being between sun and moon, winter and summer, war and peace, satiety and want -- not unlike the way Nietzsche would later speak of beyond good and evil.19 The Hindu text, Brahmanah Parimarah, tells of "holy power" (Brahman) as being discovered in moments between lightning and rain, rain and moon, moon and sun, sun and hearthfire.20 In The Republic Plato tells about a metaxy, an "intermediate realm," where one finds soul (psyche). And in The Symposium he uses the same term to locate the topos of Love (Eros).21 Pascal spoke of man's true existence as being between two infinites, the infinitely great and the infinitely small,22 and more recently Martin Heidegger has used the words Zwischen and Zwischenfall to describe the position or perspective in which an authentic poetic self finds itself.23 So also Martin Buber used the word Zwischenmenchliche to describe the authentic stance between Thou and I.24 And finally, Henry Corbin has charted the realm of the imaginal from the perspective of Persian mysticism as that of 'alam al-mithal, the mundus imaginalis, a realm between the intelligible and sensibles.25 The testimony abounds: Life, Truth, Love, Soul, God and the God beyond God appear authentically in the perspective of the between. Height is seen with depth, as if indeed "the way up and the way down are one and the same."26

The Christian doctrine of the descensus christi, focussing on and filling in the "middle," as it does, calls forth this testimony, a testimony which deepens seeing and saying with a hermeneutic of the between. Such is a perspective from Christian theology which because the perspective is pervasive of all life, rejects what Jung accepts psychologically: namely, that the descensus is merely a "stage." Theology's perspective, on the other hand, accepts what Hillman rejects: namely, the theology of Christ's descent, for without this motif theology would lose depth from its content and its perspective. It is Christian theology which puts the "between" in the motif of descensus ad inferos.

But if this theological viewing of the descensus goes beyond, or better, between Jung's christianism and Hillman's anti-christianism it does so in the name of a Christianity which is in accord with that which both Jung and Hillman agree upon: namely, the importance of deepening and darkening the study of religion and its imagery, giving it body and soul, a relatedness to the here and now, to the "middle of this dark life" where we all in fact live, not between life and death, but between death and life.

So it was that William Blake once signed a friend's autograph album with this signature: "William Blake, born 28 November 1757 in London, and has died several times since."27 St. Paul was even more emphatic, saying, "Why am I in peril every hour? . . . I die every day"28 Is this not tantamount to saying that there is a _descensus ad inferos_ every time there is a defeat for the ego, and that every time there is a defeat for the ego there is an opportunity for a deeper perspective, for a new and richer life lived _in the depths_?29

Eugene O'Neill has one of his characters in _The Hairy Ape_ say it this way:

> I ain't on earth and I ain't in heaven, get me? I'm in the middle tryin' to separate 'em. Maybe dat's what dey call hell, huh?30

NOTES

1. C. G. Jung, Collected Works, 18, p. 38.

2. Ibid.

3. Viz. Jung, Collected Works, 12, p. 227.

4. Jung, Collected Works, 13, p. 50; 14, p. 180; 9,i, p. 13, etc.

5. Jung, Collected Works, 12, pp. 306, 353, etc. It is a standard "move" by Jung to affirm strongly for psychological use a Christian image or symbol, but then to decry its one-sided rationalistic, which is to say, unpsychological interpretation by the orthodox tradition. Then, by drawing on myth and fairy tale, gnosticism and alchemy, hermeticism and astrology, Jung re-visions the interpretation, adding to the transpersonal pleroma the missing or repressed dimensions, such as Evil, the Feminine, etc. For a typical instance of this, see his essay "Aion," Collected Works, 9,ii.

6. Cf. the author's charting of Jung's work as providing a therapy (a "making whole") of theology's one-sidedness in various Eranos lectures (1975, 1977, 1978, 1980, 1981, 1982) and in the book, Christs: Meditations on Archetypal Images in Christian Theology, Volume I (New York: Seabury, 1981).

7. Tertullian, De anima, 55; cf. Hillman, Dream and the Underworld (New York: Harper, 1979), p. 85. Hillman does notice that Tertullian is here describing the position of others that he does not himself hold.

8. Hillman, loc. cit.

9. For another view of this matter of "depth" in relation to Christian theology, see the author's "The Two Sandals of Christ: Descent into History and into Hell," Eranos 1981 (Frankfurt: Insel Verlag, 1982), pp. 147ff, especially footnote 96

where the difference between the present author and Hillman is articulated.

10. This is even more clear in a chapter against Christianity in _Inter Views_ (New York: Harper & Row, 1983), Chapter 5.

11. Now published in book-form as _The Myth of Analysis_ (New York: Harper, 1972), p. 187.

12. Hillman, _Re-visioning Psychology_ (New York: Harper, 1975), p. 207.

13. _Dream and the Underworld_, p. 46.

14. Jung, _Collected Works_, 18, p. 38.

15. Cited in Heinz-Jurgen Vogels, _Christi Abstieg in Totenreich und das Lauterungsgericht in den Toten_ (Freiburg: Herder, 1976), p. 5.

16. W. Bousset, _Kyrios Christos_ (Gottingen, 1921), p. 60.

17. J. Pohle, _Lehrbuch der Dogmatick_ (1902), cited by Herbert Vorgrimler, "Christ's Descent into Hell--Is it Important?" _Concilium_, I, 2 (1966), 76f.

18. J. Galot, "La descente du Christ aux enfers," _Nouvelle revue theologique_, LXXXIII (1961), 472.

19. Heraclitus, fragment #67 (D-K).

20. For this text, see Heinrich Zimmer, _Philosophies of India_, ed. Campbell (New York: Meridian, 1961), pp. 66-74.

21. _Republic_, X; _cf_. Miller, _Christs_, chapter 25.

22. _Pensees_, #72.

23. _Existence and Being_ (Chicago: Regnery, 1949), p. 288; _Einfuhrung in die Metaphysik_ (Tubingen: Niemeyer, 1953), pp. 124f; _etc_.

24. _Viz_. Buber, _Between Man and Man_, tr. Smith (New York: Macmillan, 1965), pp. 98, 203f.

25. Henry Corbin, "_Mundus imaginalis_, or the

Imaginary and the Imaginal," _Spring 1972_, 1-19;
"Pour une charte de l'imaginal," _Corps spirituel
et terre celeste_ (Deuxieme edition; Paris:
ditions Buchet/Chastel, 1979), _prelude_. And
compare the present author's treatment of this
motif of "the between" in relation to a theology
of the Trinity, in "Between God and the
Gods--Trinity," _Eranos 1980_ (Frankfurt: Insel
Verlag, 1981), pp. 81ff.

26. Heraclitus, fragment #60 (D-K).

27. Cited by Gerhard Adler, "Remembering and
Forgetting," _Panarion Conference_ 1976, tape (Los
Angeles: The Panarion Foundation, 1976).

28. I Corinthians 15:30f.

29. _Cf._ Jung, _Collected Works_, 14, p. 546: ". . .
the experience of the Self is always a defeat for
the ego."

30. Eugene O'Neill, _The Emperor Jones_, _Anna Christie_,
and The Hairy Ape (New York: Modern Library,
1937), p. 258.

MARY and WALTER BRENNEMAN are operators of a dairy farm in Marshfield, Vermont. Walter, Assistant Professor of Religion at the University of Vermont is the author of _Spirals, A Study in Symbol, Myth and Ritual_, and co-author of _The Seeing Eye, Hermeneutical Phenomenology in the Study of Religion_.

JAMES GOSS is Professor of Religious Studies at California State University, Northridge, and has published articles on Albert Camus, process thought, Flannery O'Connor, and is currently working on an introduction to the Bible for freshmen.

JAMES A. HALL, M.D., is a Jungian analyst trained at the C. G. Jung Institute in Zurich, and a founding member and past-president of the Inter-Regional Society of Jungian Analysts, clinical Associate Professor of Psychiatry at the University of Texas Health Center at Dallas, and a consultant to the internship program at Perkins School of Theology, Southern Methodist University. He is the author of _Jungian Dream Interpretation: A Handbook of Theory and Practice_.

PETER HOMANS is Associate Professor of Religion and Psychological Studies in the Divinity School at the University of Chicago. He is the author of _Theology after Freud_, the editor of and a contributor to _Childhood and Selfhood: Essays on Tradition, Religion and Modernity in the Psychology of Erik H. Erikson_, and the author of _Jung in Context_.

LUTHER H. MARTIN is Associate Professor and Chairman of the Religion Department at The University of Vermont. He is an editor of and contributor to _Techologies of the Self: A Seminar with Michel Foucault_, and is completing a book on Hellenistic religions.

DAVID L. MILLER is Watson-Ledden Professor of Religion at Syracuse University. Since 1975 he has been a member of the Eranos Circle in Switzerland, and he is the author of _Gods and Games, The New Polytheism_, and _Christs_.

MOKUSEN MIYUKI is Professor of Religious Studies at California State University, Northridge; a faculty member of the Institute of Buddhist studies, Berkeley; a faculty member of the C. G. Jung Institute of Los Angeles; a Jungian analyst and a Buddhist Priest. He is the author of *Kreisen des Lichtes: Die Erfahrung der Goldenen Blute*.

THOMAS MOORE is Director of Psychological Studies at the Dallas Institute of Humanities and Culture, and has a private practice of psychotherapy in Dallas. He has just completed a book entitled *Sacred Fantasy: Re-Imagining the Practice of Religion*, and is working on a book on the Marquis de Sade.

WILLIAM PADEN is Associate Professor of Religion at The University of Vermont. He is working on a book on the comparative study of religion.

WAYNE G. ROLLINS is Professor of Religious Studies, the Co-ordinator of the Graduate Program in Religious Studies, and the Director of the Ecumenical Institute at Assumption College. He is the author of *The Gospels: Portraits of Christ* and of *Jung and the Bible*.

ANN BELFORD ULANOV is a Jungian Analyst, a member of the Board of Directors of the C. G. Jung Institute in New York City, and Professor of Psychiatry and Religion, Union Theological Seminary. She is the author of *The Feminine in Christian Theology and in Jungian Psychology*; *Receiving Woman: Studies in the Psychology and Theology of the Feminine*; and with her husband, Barry Ulanov, *Religion and the Unconscious*; *Primary Speech: A Psychology of Prayer*; and *Cinderella and Her Sisters: The Envied and the Envying*.